SOCIAL AND ECONOMIC DEVELOPMENT IN NORTH-EAST INDIA

SOCIAL AND ECONOMIC DEVELOPMENT IN NORTH-EAST INDIA

EDITED BY
SHASHI AHLUWALIA

GYAN PUBLISHING HOUSE
New Delhi - 110002

SOCIAL AND ECONOMIC
DEVELOPMENT
IN
NORTH-EAST INDIA

ISBN :9788121203388

Published in 2015 in India by
Gyan Publishing House
23, Ansari Road, Daryaganj,
New Delhi - 110002
Phones : 23261060, 23282060 Fax : 23285914
e-mail : books@gyanbooks.com
website : gyanbooks.com

Laser Typesetting at : Vinayak Printers, Delhi
Printed at : Salasar Imaging System, Delhi

MEENAKSHI, SHOBHANA
and
RAJESH

PREFACE

The North East is much more than a geographical concept, a track of land which is part of India. There is much more to it than is understood by most of us. There is a lack of awareness on the streak of individuality which marks the terrain. For, it has its varied culture, socio-economic problems, racial variations and ethnic diversities. Collectively, it provides a colourful spectrum of the rainbow that India is. Yet, within this spectrum, there are seven different strands—Assam, Meghalaya, Tripura, Manipur, Nagaland, Mizoram and Arunachal Pradesh.

It is this spectrum which is under analysis in this book. Assam has a heary tradition, a long history, an exotic scanerio. The people are, by and large, peace-loving, content to live in their native settings, ekeing a living from land, letting life drift on without tension. Yet the land was under pressure from immigrants, most of them illegal. The resultant tension created a problem, the like of which Assam had never faced. Mercifully, an accord has been hammered out between the Government of India and the Assam agitation leaders and normalcy is returning to the State. The State is now getting back on the rails. There are probloms in Nagaland, Mizoram and Manipur where there is growing feeling that the people are yet to be drawn into the mainstream of India. There is also militants who are out to accentuate differences and to excerbate feelings and to sow seeds of dissension. However, such elements are getting isolated.

The turmoil on the surface does not, in reality, indicate any deep fission. The people, by and large, have time only for work or play......work in the fields, raising the crops, work in foraging for fuel, and play which includes dancing and singing and roaming around enjoying the pristine glory of nature, getting close to the flora and fauna of the area, thanking one's stars for letting the area look green and verdant and colourful all through the year,

There are developments coming to the area. Modernity is slowly but surely making its presence felt. But there is a great deal of attention to avoid modernity ruining the native grace and poise and richness. Every bridge that is erected, every factory that is set up takes note of the ecological factor. Education is being taken to remote corners where thick forests make transport highly difficult. Roads are being built, communication channels improved, contacts being maintained to remove the sense of isolation among the people of the area.

The strategy of development, which is seen in action in the North East, is indeed impressive. More funds are being pumped in to hasten the pace of progress.

It is in this context that the present book gains significance. It is the aim of the authors to throw some light on the area, to provide an arm-chair trip through the exotic land, to introduce the readers to the variety that makes the whole of the North East such an inspiring part of India, to bring to them the efforts which are being made to modernise the area without changing its basic character and to remove prevailing air of remoteness about the place. The authors hope that they have succeeded in this objective.

The authors are grateful to the contributors for their articles and also to various newspapers and journals and to the Publications Division, Government of India for permission to reproduce material from their publications.

The authors are also grateful to Prof. K. Swaminathan and S/Shri V. Narayanswamy, J.P. Uniyal and R.K. Murthi who had been kind enough to give many useful suggestions.

CONTENTS

LIST OF ILLUSTRATIONS

1. Mrs. Indira Gandhi, Former Prime Minister, wearing Assam head dress

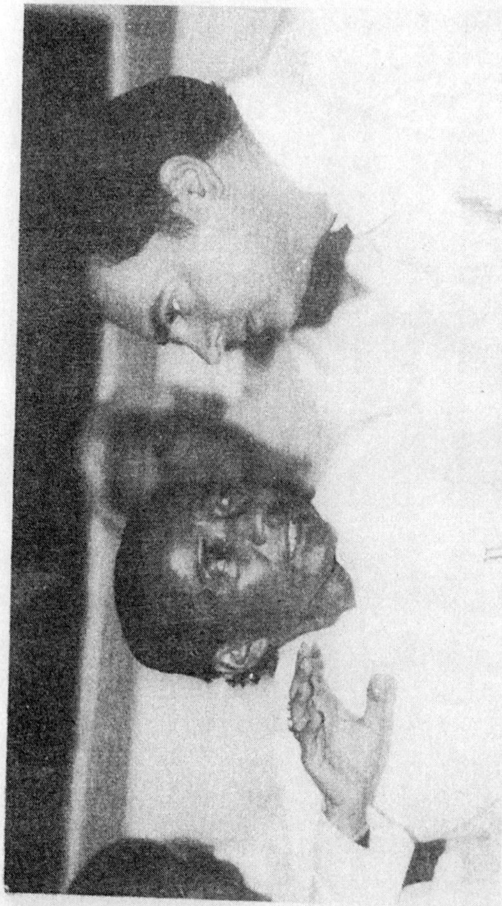

2. Mr. Rajiv Gandhi with Hiteshwar Saikia, Chief Minister of Assam

3A. Mr. Giani Zail Singh with Mr. Hiteshwar Saikia

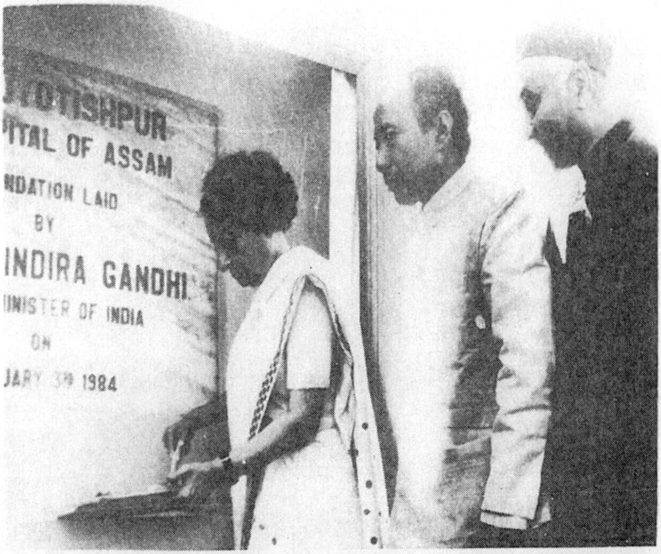

3B Mrs. Indira Gandhi, the then Prime Minister, laying the foundation stone of the capital of Assam

4. Assam builds her new capital

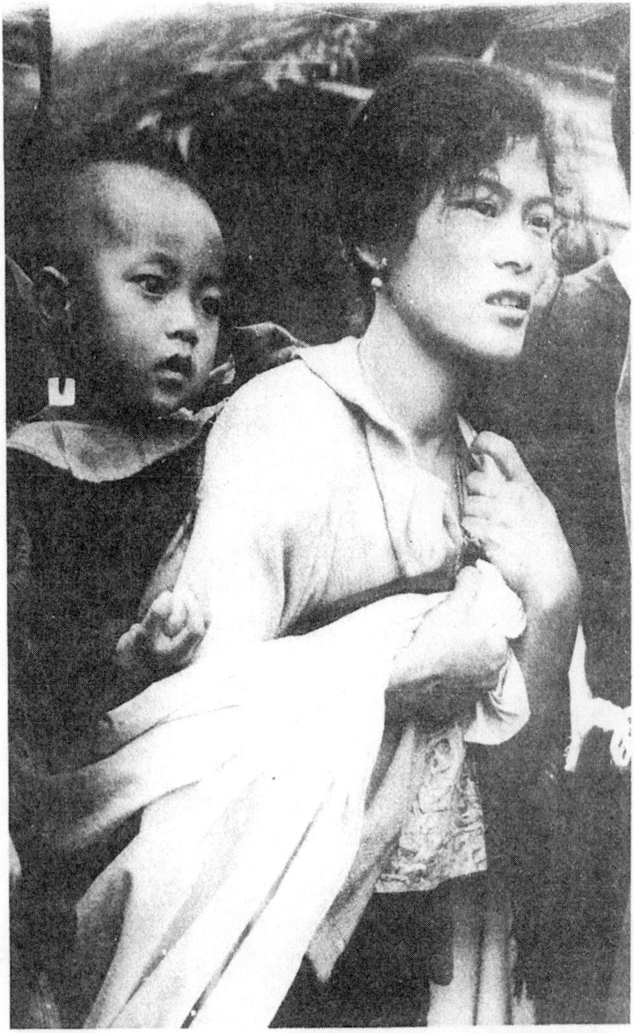

5. A Nagaland woman carrying her child

6. 'A Songong (war drum) of Nagaland

7. A Nishi farmer of Arunachal Pradesh

8A. A Miji woman of Arunachal Pradesh

8B. Two woman of Meghalaya

1
INTRODUCTION

by
Shashi Ahluwalia

"The North-East region has over 26 million people of heterogeneous ethnic groups spread over a difficult terrain. There are five fullfeldged States in it, namely, Assam, Manipur, Tripura, Nagaland and Meghalaya and two Union Territories, Arunachal Pradesh and Mizoram.

The region's main problem is economic backwardness, accentuated by the woeful lack of communications.

If the accumulated agony of the people is to be alleviated, the only way out is to give top priority to the region's economic needs, like harnessing its abundant natural resources with single-minded devotion. The setting up of the North-East Council was a signal break-through. Since its inception, the Council has proved its utility in taking up schemes to develop power, rail and road communication in the region.

ASSAM

The land of rising sun, perpetually hovering clouds, blue hills and the ever green plains, Assam manifests all the diversities and characteristics of a miniature India. The strategic location of the State, its varied resources and the glorious heritage of the people have secured for Assam a unique place in the geography, history and socio-political life of India. Dcwn the centuries Assam served as a gateway for succeeding streams of races entering into India from the South-East and the Far East of this continent. It is through this State also that the Indo-Gangetic civilization transcended to the scores of islands of the eastern Pacific. Indian mythology and the epics are replete with glorious references about the heroic exploits of the monarchs of Kamarupa. Sonitpur and Kundilnagar and the beauty and the brilliance of the princesses of this area like Rukmini, Usha, Ulupi and Hidimba. The daughter of the Kamarupa King, Bhagaddatta had the distinction of becoming the Empress of India through her marriage with the Chief of the Kauravas.

Even in the recorded history Kamarupa's Bhaskaravarma of the 7th century was accorded the highest honour in the reception at the conference of the Indian Kings convened by Harshavardhana. The advent of the Ahoms in 1228 A.D. and their successful and uninterrupted administration spreading over 600 years brought stability to this region and earned special fame for excellence of culture and economic achievement. The advent of Aryan civilization into the plains of Assam dating back to 400 B C. consolidated the links with the rest of the country. The Aryans, however, never entered Assam as conquerors, as a result of which this area has been able to remain free from a number of scourges that marked the Aryan way of life in the rest of the country. The most outstanding feature in Assam is the lack of caste rigorousness and total absence of untouchability. Evils of Hindu society like Suttie and dowry have been virtually absent in Assam.

When Assam passed into the hands of the British in 1826, it had already witnessed a series of natural and political catastrophes causing a virtual breakdown of its economic life, and bringing in its trail social strains on its population. Over a million Assamese were killed during the Civil War that rocked the State from 1776 to the close of the 18th century. While the beginning of the 19th century witnessed one of the most harrowing invasions from Burma, when lakhs of people were butchered or were driven out of the State, the close of the 19th century witnessed repeated outbreaks of epidemics like Kala Azaar and Cholera, which denuded a district like Nowgong of one third of its population. A series of earthquakes and floods in the 18th and 19th centuries almost crippled the economy of the State.

During the pre-independence era Assam lagged far behind the rest of the country in respect of developmental activities. The railway lines were laid in Assam in the 1880's but vast areas were left untouched by railways till the advent of freedom.

The partition of the country added to the complexity of Assam's problems. With the separation of eastern Bengal to constitute what was then called East Pakistan, Assam lost her direct outlet to the sea and to the main land through dependable surface and sea routes.

INDUSTRY

Assam is rich in mineral wealth. It holds a unique position in the production of mineral oil. Other minerals found in the State are coal, limestone, refractory clay, dolomite and natural gas.

Of the agriculture based industries, tea occupies an important place. There are nearly 750 tea plantations in the State. Petroleum and petroluem products form the other main industries. Assam produces about 50 per cent of the country's total petroluem output and natural gas. The State has two oil refineries and the third, with a petro-chemical complex, is under way. There is also a public sector fertilizer factory in Namrup. Other industries are sugar, jute, silk, paper, plywood manufacture and rice and oil miling. Important cottage industries are handloom, sericulture, manufacture of cane and bamboo articles, carpentry, smithy and manufacture of brass utensils. The pace of industrialisation in the State has been boosted up significantly with the setting up of five District Industries Centres (DIC). An export-oriented handloom project has been started at Sualkuchi to exploit the export potentialities of Eri and Muga.

IRRIGATION AND POWER

The two medium irrigation schemes started in the State during the Third Five Year Plan and which spilled over to the Fourth Plan were the Yamuna and Sukla irrigation projects. The two projects have already been commissioned. At present there are four medium and more than 200 minor irrigation projects in the State. Execution of one major, nine medium and 218 minor projects has started. It has been decided to develop a gross irrigation coverage of 7.67 lakh hectares of land against a total not crop area of 31.76 lakh hectares in the State. New power projects are under construction at Lakwa and Bongaigaon.

TEA INDUSTRY OF ASSAM

Assam is the 'tea country' of India. Tea is the principal cash crop of the State and one of the main export items of India. Our country produces about 30 per cent of the total world produce and its share in the export market is about 28 per cent. India is the biggest producer and biggest exporter of tea in the world. Of this 53 per cent is produced in Assam and its contribution to the national exchequer as foreign exchange earner is 60 per cent of the total. At present there are some 750 tea gradens in Assam with 1,89,000 hectares of planted area. In 1980 tea production of the area was 305 million kg. as against India's total of 575 million kg. Besides contributing handsomely to the central excise coffer, the tea industry is the biggest labour-oriented industry of Assam Moreover to cater to the different needs of the industry, other ancilliary industries grew up which in the course of time, blossomed into independent industries. Thus tea has played a very important role in the socio-economic life of the State.

LABOUR INTENSIVE INDUSTRY

Tea is highly labour intensive industry employing 3.46 lakh men and 3.60 lakh women (their biggest single avenue of organised employment) and 85 thousand others (adolescents and children), it provides year-round employments. Moreover in the peak tea season, 3 to 4 lakh temporary labourers are hired. Over 18 lakh workers get employment through other ancilliary industries.

Originally, the labourers had to be brought from Orissa, Madhya Pradesh, Andhra Pradesh and Chotanagpur area of Bihar to work in the land. Through the years these people have merged with the local scene. Today their descendents play an important role in the socio-economic and political life of Assam. The living condition, wages, various facilities, have also improved and the children go to school to get education; some of them are going for higher studies also. In 1955, the Assam Tea Plantations Provident Fund Scheme was introduced as a part of social security measures.

DEVELOPMENT OF COMMUNICATION SYSTEM

The Britishers first entered Assam mainly by the river-way of the Brahmaputra. For a long time even in this country, there was steamer service between Gauhati and Calcutta. It was originally opened to cater for the needs of tea gardens to carry machinery, consumer goods, post, etc. Afterwards it could not serve the expanding tea industry and developing the roadways and Railways became necessary.

Faced with the difficulty of commuting and collecting the tea produced, roads were constructed to connect the farflung gardens. A look at the two Trunk Roads of Assam on both the banks of the Brahmaputra shows that the tea gardens are situated at either side of main highways and the artery roads.

ANCILLARY INDUSTRIES

Not only did tea become a top priority industry within a short span of time it also helped the development of some ancillary industries which in the long run became self-sufficient and independent industries. As a first example we can point out plywood industry. Originally started to manufacture tea chests (The Assam Saw Mill and Timber Company was floated in 1918) and now it is one of the established industries of India.

The requirements of tea machinery led to manufacturing units in Calcutta. Today India is self-sufficient in this respect and also exports these to other countries earning substantial amount of foreign exchange. Aluminium foil, tinplate, metal fittings, paper card board and fertilisers are other industries providing employment directly or indirectly connected with tea production.

No doubt tea is the major industry of Assam. 11 per cent of the State's revenue comes from tea. Assam alone produces 30 per cent of the world's total production, more than 50 per cent of India's and 67 per cent of the North East India's, thus becoming the single biggest producer of tea. Tea plantations do not encourage soil erosion and do not disturb ecological balance which has become a modern day problem in many spheres. Besides the sloping land used up by the gardens are not suitable for other cultivations. If not successfully planted with tea bushes, it would have remained fallow or a jungle only. The gardens also provide scope for local concated population to find 'white collar' jobs as clerks, typists, etc. The districts of Lakhimpur, Dibrugarh, Sibsagar, Darrang in the Brahmaputra valley and Cachar District in the south contain most of the gardens. Among them Dibrugarh District produces the best tea. Assam tea liquor is strong and Darjeeling tea is famous for its aroma. After Independence most of the gardens have been bought by the Indians.

EXPORT INDUSTRY

Tea is mainly an export industry. India exports tea to some 50 countries earning substantial amount of foreign exchange. Besides the major importers U.K. and U.S.S.R. West Germany, Netherlands, Poland, U.S.A., Canada, Australia, New Zealand, Japan, Egypt, Tunisia, Iraq, Iran, etc. also import our tea. Climaticially, Assam is highly suitable for cultivation of tea. The tea industry must not be allowed to stagnate or be neglected as other tea-exporting countries like Sri Lanka, China are providing strong competition in the foreign market. Of late, the industry has been afflicted by other problems of high cost of production, fall in quality, etc. the transport bottleneck is another problem. As the Broad Gauge is yet to reach Gauhati, the main outlet for the hinterland of tea, the cost of transport (mainly by the road) is high and until the Broad Gauge railway is opened the problem will persist. Some gardens are so old, especially in the Cachar District that new plantation is necessary as no amount of proning can revive its productivity. This again calls for sizeable amount of investment.

AUCTION MARKET OF GAUHATI

After much clamour, the long overdue Auction Market was opened at Gauhati in September 970. This has given a boost to the local tea planters and has been able to attract foreign buyers and sometimes record price too. From the total of 22 million kg. tea sold in 1971-72 in the Gauhati Auction sales increased to 69.8 million kg. in 1979-80. Thus without having to commute Calcutta and saving considerable transport cost and avoiding the Calcutta Tea Entry Tax, the tea planters of the region are getting the benefit. Export of tea through Kandla in the West Coast has increased in the recent past as the port-duty is less there as compared to Calcutta and the authorities arrange for speedy storage and disposal (Economic Survey of Assam 1970). Dr. Amiya K. Paul in his article "Role of the Tea Plantation Industry in the Economic Development of North-East India" suggests two auction centres—one for internal consumption of tea in India and the other for the foreign market which will promote export and will bring higher price for quality tea. Dr. Paul also suggests setting up of a fertilizer plant in Gauhati with a capacity of 100 tonnes per day as the one at Namrup cannot cater for the agriculture sector and the giant tea sector.

In conclusion it can be said that the demand for tea is not likely to fall as it is a major beverage of the world with two thirds of its population drinking it. Efforts to improve its quality through research and marketing it with a special eye on the foreign market must be kept up so that this major industry does not lose out to other countries. After all a small country like Sri Lanka can surprise us by leading in the tourism development in Asia leaving behind a much more potential India. In this context, the Tea Board and the Tea Trading Corporation of India have a vital role to play.

Specially those knowhow, machinery, raw material and, if necessary, finance should be made available. Besides the traditional markets, efforts should be made to woo the buyers from the new drinking areas of the world. "Such a service at the garden level will change the whole economy of tea in India" and the land of the 'two leaves and a bud' can retain its promising position.

MANIPUR

AGRICULTURE

The main occupation of 66 per cent of the population of Mainpur is agriculture. Nearly 92 per cent of the total land area is hilly and covered by forests. Forest reserves are being developed by planting better species of timber. Bamboo is found in large quantities. In the Jiri and Barak river drainage area alone bamboos cover an estimated area of 2,585 sq. km. yielding 3,00,000 tonnes annually. Main crop is paddy, while wheat and maize are also grown in some areas. Orchards are also being set up.

INDUSTRY

The State has no large scale industry. Handloom weaving is the largest single cottage industry. Other cottage industries are sericulture, bamboo and cane articles, carpentry, blacksmithy leather goods, edible oil crushing, rice milling, gur and Khandsari.

To accelerate the development of small scale industries, an industrial advisory board has been set up and the jurisdiction of Assam Financial Corporation extended to Manipur. At Takyelpat near Imphal, an industrial estate is being set up.

IRRIGATION AND POWER

Irrigation is done through minor irrigation works by constructing weirs across running streams for better distribution of water during the monsoons. Loktak is the only major power project in the State.

MEGHALAYA

AGRICULTURE

Over 80 per cent of the people of Meghalaya are engaged in agricultural pursuits. Irrigated area is about 27 per cent of the cultivated area. The principal crops are potato, tez-pata, sugarcane, oilseeds, cotton, jute, mesta and arecanut. Selected areas have been earmaked for growing high-yielding varieties of paddy, wheat and maize. In the Khasi and Jaintia Hills districts fruits and vegetables are also grown and special programmes have been undertaken to develop horticulture. The production of foodgrains is around 1,30,000 tonnes annually. The annual production of cash crops is estimated to be : Jute 50,000 bales, potato 71,000 tonnes and tapioca 5,000 tonnes. The state is making good progress in horticulture. It produces a'out 70,000 tonnes of pineapples, 80,000 tonnes of oranges and 35,000 tonnes of bananas annually.

INDUSTRY

The mineral wealth of the Khasi Hills, Jaintia Hills and Garo Hills districts includes coal, sillimanite, limestone, dolomite, fire clay, felspar, quartz and glass sand. Ninetyfive per cent of India's total output of sillimanite is produced in the Khasi Hillls District. The Garo Hills District has deposits of coal, limestone, fire clay and light coloured sand-stone. The estimated reserves of coal in the State are about 12,000 lakh tonnes.

The Cement factory at Cherrapunjee produces 590 tonnes of clinker and 605 tonnes of cement daily. The capacity of this factory is being extended to 955 tonnes of cement daily. A timber treatment plant is being set up at Daruggiri in Garo Hills. Several mineral-based industries are coming up. A plywood factory and a beverages factory have already been set up.

IRRIGATION AND POWER

There are at present four hydel projects with a total installed capacity of 125.2 mw. In addition to this there is a micro hydle station of 1.5 mw capacity at Shillong.

NAGALAND

AGRICULTURE

Agriculture is the main occupation of 90 per cent of the population of Nagaland. Rice is the only important foodgrain grown in the State. The total area operated for cultivation is 6,80,000 hectares. The total terraced rice cultivated area with irrigation is 38,000 hectares.

Forests cover 17.56 per cent of the area of the State and they contribute considerably to the revenue.

INDUSTRY

There is a sugar mill with a crushing capacity of 1,200 tonnes per day at Dimapur. The Nagaland Forest Products Ltd. at Tijit has gone into production. A paper mill with a production capacity of 100 tonnes per day and a distillery unit at Dimapur are being set up. A factory for the production of decorative and commercial plywood is also coming up. Handloom and secirulture are the important cottage industries. There are six weaving-cum-production centres, five sericulture farms, one handicraft training-cum-production centre and three small scale industries service centres.

IRRIGATION AND POWER

Minor irrigation works in the State are mostly meant to divert small hill streamlets to irrigate valleys used for rice cultivation. Total installed capacity of power upto date is 3.17 mw. Out of 964 villages in Nagaland, the number of electrified villages till now is 275.

MIZORAM

AGRICULTURE

About 90 per cent of the people of Mizoram are engaged in agricultural pursuits. Out of about 60,000 families, 50,000 families are in agriculture, cf which 10,000 are in the process of permanent settlement and 40,000 are still continuing shift cultivation. At present 5 per cent of total area is under cultivation and a little over 1.5 per cent is made permanent cultivation. Irrigated area forms seven per cent of the total cultivated area. In the hill slopes maize and paddy are cultivated. Other crops grown are pulses. sugarcane, chillies, ginger, tobacco, vegetables, turmeric, potato, banana and pineapple. Shift cultivation is ordinarily practised though terrace rice cultivation and Wet rice cultivation practices have been taken up in recent years.

Nearly two thirds of the area of the territory is covered with forests. Important forest products are timber, bamboo and *agar*.

INDUSTRY

There is no major industry in Mizoram. Handloom and handicrafts are the cottage industries. Rice milling, oil and flour milling, mechanised bamboo workshops, saw milling, brick making, aluminium casting and furniture workshops are some of the small industries which have been established. A survey conducted in 1973-74 has established that there is sufficient raw material for estabilishing a paper-pulp project.

IRRIGATION AND POWER

Schemes like the cementing for water points construction of small reservoirs at the collection points in the streams or springs and some improvised way of bringing water as near the villages as possible are being implemented. Irrigation is difficult because of the mountainous terrain.

There are seven diesel power stations to generate electricity mainly for domestic consumption at Aizwal, Lunglei, Lawngtlai, Champhai and Hnahthial. The total power generation capacity is estimated to be about 1,876 kw.

TRIPURA

About 60 per cent of the area is under forests. Total sown area in the State is 245.9 thousand hectares and total gross cropped area is 392.3 thousand hectares. The net irrigated area is only 11.9 thousand hectares, *i.e.* about 4.8

per cent of net sown area. Rice, Jute, mesta, potatoes, oilseeds, wheat, pulses, sugarcane and cotton are the main crops.

Tea is the major industry in Tripura. Tea plantations cover an area of about 5,600 hectares at the end of 1979-80. The annual production of processed tea was about 46 lakh kg. Important cottage industries are handlooms, handicrafts and khadi. There are 89 weavers' societies and 88 handicrafts and carpentry societies.

Some major industries are proposed to be set up in the State. They include a paper mill and a jute mill. Establishment of the jute mill has made substantial progress. The number of private sector industries undr small scale industry scheme are 1,221 and those of public sector industries are 23.

Between 1978 and 1980, 125 river-lift irrigation schemes were taken up, 200 shallow tube-wells were Sunk, 15 deep tube-wells were installed in different parts of the State. One medium irrigation project over river Gomati was taken up in December, 1980. During this period, irrigation potential has been raised from 3,875 hectares to 9,125 hectares.

Once a visitor descends on the sacred soil of Tripura, his exist will entirely depend, as is a popular belief in Tripura, on the will of Tripurasundari, the reigning deity of the sacred land. The superstition obviously makes sense when even the casual visitor to Tripura is captivated by the charm of this land. The charm of Agartala, the capital town, lies in the rhythmic blending in it of the classical and the modern. The old monuments standing amidst the thronging bazar present a strange sight. The Ujjayanta palace, however, stands out with distinction. Reminiscent of a royal dynasty, which held sway over a great Tripura for an uninterrupted thousand years the palace presents a grand synthesis of different architectural styles The main entrance is flanked by two patches of water with the intervening space presenting a replica of a Mughal garden.

The Kunjaban palace, at a stone's throw from the Circuit House has been converted into the Governor's House one with a difference though. The antiquity of its structure too takes one down the memory lane into those days of royal grandeur. The palace is also associated with the memories of poet Rabindranath who composed here some of his finest lyrics, during his stay with the Tripura Monarch.

The rectangular shaped Jagannath temple, in the vicinity of the Ujjayanta palace, is octogonal at the basement with a pradakshina path round the sanctum. The temple draws a constant stream of devotees who stream also to the nearby Uma Maheswar temple. The lake-garlanded Maharaja Bir Bikram College campus, the Kunjaban lake and the shy Howrah river which flows past the town gently are worth seeing. The well arranged State Museum near a busy street corner provides another peep to the State's past.

Eight kilometre drive by taxi or town bus from Agartala will take one to the famous Chaturdash Devta temple on the bank of the Howrah. The temple believed to have been constructed during the Mahabharata age, houses fourteen gods and goddesses, made of an alloy of eight sacred metals. July, however, is the proper time to visit the temple, when people from all over the State assemble there for the week long kharchi puja, and the ker puja, a fortnight later. The latter occasion is marked by colourful dances.

Another spectacular edifice, the Nirmahal, on the vast expanse of the big lake, Rudrasagar, is 49 kilometres away by road from Agartala. The lake offers ample opportunities for different aquatic sports, while the palace itself is ideal for picnic in unusual surroundings. One, who rows away from the Nirmahal in the evening, will never forget the grandeur of the enchanted building against the backdrop of a setting sun. The secluded inspection bungalow at Kakrabon at the terminus of a few minutes' drive from Nirmahal, can accommodate the tourist who is reluctant to go back without enjoying the moonlit spectacle as well.

The lake-dotted Udaipur town is only 14 kilometres away from Kakrabon. The famous temple of Tripurasundari, known as Matar bari in popular parlance, is only a kilometre off from Udaipur town. Claimed to be one of the fiftyone pithasthanas, the temple area pulstate with reverberating chantings and crowd of devotees. The temple with an artificial lake nearby, is about five centuries old. Six hours drive from Agartala by bus or car will take the visitor to Unakuti, the hill-top pilgrimage, where rock cut gods and goddesses have been nestling since the Buddhist times. It is only six kilometres off from Kailasahar, the sub-divisional town with modestly priced accommodation facilities, which can also be approached by air from Agartala.

One needs to drive only a hundred and ten hilly kilometres to find out the source of Gomati river, which plays a vital role in Rabindranath's lyric drama, 'Bisarjan'. The foamy symphony of the Dumbur falls has inspired more poetry in Tripura. This source of the Gomati also known as Tirthamukh, draws legion people during the Uttarayan Samkranti, the occasion for a big fair. A magnificent temple of resergent Tripura, the inspection bungalow at Amarpur, 21 kilometres away, overlooking a big lake should be visited either for accommodation or sheer pleasure of sight seeing.

Whichever season one motors up the hill slopes to the eastern gringe of the Jampuitang range, one lands there in spring time. The unrivalled beauty of the land of eternal spring spiced with the murmuring streams and the exquisite wild frangrance, is a wholly diverting experience.

A visit to an interior village, with treetop tongi houses and the colourful tribals in the fields, can offer a different kind of holiday. Some tribal villages are very close to the capital town itself. The visitor will also come by deer, rabbits and different species of birds all over the State.

And before saying goodbye to this magic land, the visitor will have enough souvenirs to pick up from. It can be anythin ; a wooden lamp stand or an ivory doll, a *dubri*, the colourful garment, or a *riya* the magnificent breastwear for ladies, or a flower ornament. Or it can be the innocent smile of the Tripuri maiden which hangs on air long after she walked out of sight, or the rhythm of the Reang dancers' steps, which resounds in your ears even after the dancers retire. It can be the nostalgic memory of the famous Tippers flute floating across hills and dales in the eerie mid day silence.

ARUNACHAL PRADESH

AGRICULTURE

Nearly 46 per cent of the population of Arunachal Pradesh is engaged in agriculture. Irrigated area forms 17 per cent of the total cultivated area of about 14,000 hectares. The traditional method of agriculture is jhumming, a kind of shifting cultivation. Main crops are rice, maize, millets, wheat and mustard. Forest covers 61,000 sq. km. of the area.

The horticultural potential in Arunachal Pradesh is noted very high. Banana, citrus and pineapple below 3,000 feet, peach, plum, pears and apricot upto 5.000 and apple plum, cherries, walnuts, almonds and hazelnuts, etc. above 5,000 feet are grown in three out of five districts of Arunachal Pradesh.

INDUSTRY

Principal industries are forest-based medium and small industries established include saw mills, plywood and veneering mills, rice mills, and preservation units, oil expellers, besides handloom and handicraft industries. The government is providing training facilities in various trades under cottage industries as well as technical education through the Government Craft Training Centres and Industrial Training Institutes.

IRRIGATION AND POWER

A hydel project with an installed capacity of 750 kw. was commissioned at Rahung in 1972. Two more hydel projects at Pasighat and Basar with installed capacities of 200 kw. and 100 mw. respectively were completed in November 1973. During 1976 and 1977, Along (400 kw), Tezu (500 kw), Tiratjo-micro-hydel project (750 kw) and Tawang (1,500 kw) were commissioned. Ziro 2,000 kw), Tezu (500 kw), Dirang (1,500 kw) and Siagh Hydro-electric projects are almost ready. The total installed capacity in March 1975 was 3.4 mw. Arunachal Pradesh had only seven electrified villages in 1961 and the number increased to 61 by March 31, 1975.

2
FOCUS ON NORTH EAST

by
Indira Gandhi

The various political parts of this region are bound by several common characteristics. Their people share a variety and picturesqueness of dress and custom that is rarely equalled. If they have the good fortune to live in the midst of green and lush surroundings, nature also visits them with many hardships, torrential rains, floods and landslides. The very terrain presents formidable obstacles to communications. Roads and bridges are needed to connect one point with another and to serve the region as a whole. Rivers remain to be harnessed for common advantage. The resources of the forests and the wealth hidden in the soil must be utilised for the welfare of all.

The primary purpose of this Council is the development of the region for greater human welfare. The first principle of development is co-ordinated activity. I have no doubt that the different units of this region will gain by such co-ordinated work.

I should like to take this opportunity to remove some misconceptions regarding the scope and functioning of this Council. This is an organisation of the various political units

(Excerpts from the inaugural address by the Prime Minister. Smt. Indira Gandhi at the 1st meeting of North Eastern Council at Shillong on 7th November, 1972).

of this region, set up under an Act of Parliament, to formulate a coordinated plan for development and welfare. It is not a super-government. It does not abridge the power of the States and Union Territories in any manner whatsoever. It is not an extension of the Union Government. It is an advisory and not a supervisory body. It does not alter the relationship of the member units with the Central Government. The Central Government will not use the Council to interfere with the affairs and functioning of the various Governments of this region.

I should like the Council to draw up projects which will benefit more than one unit. There are sectors such as transport and communication, power, marketing, institutional financing, training, preparation of feasibility studies for industries, etc. in which a regional approach would be most welcome. Vision and practicability are the two key tests of good planning, I should like to assure you the suggestions made by the Council and the projects drawn up by it will be considered with particular attention by the Planning Commission and also the various Ministeries of the Government of India.

The implementation of these projects and schemes will be the charge of the respective Government and their agencies. This might entail the strengthening of their existing administrative and executive machinery. It is important that each of the North Eastern States builds up expertise in the matter of data collection, project preparation and construction of administration.

3

NORTH EASTERN COUNCIL FOR ACCELERATED ECONOMIC DEVELOPMENT

by
Prakash Mehrotra

It would be appropriate to remind ourselves of what our Prime Minister had said while inaugurating the North Eastern Council on the 7th November, 1972. She had observed : "The primary purpose of this Council is the development of the region for greater human welfare...I should like the Council to draw up projects which will benefit more than one unit...I am glad to inaugurate this Council which is a promising innovation in regional planning. May it fulfil the hope we have invested in it."

INSTRUMENTAL IN INITIATING PROGRAMMES

As I look over the progress of these ten years I am glad to say that the expectations held out by the Prime Minister have been, to a great extent, fulfilled. During this decade, not only has the Council been able to provide a forum for discussion of the common problems of the region, but it has also been instrumental in initiating major programmes for the development of the region, and has, indeed, come to be recognised as an effective Regional Planning Authority. Both the Central Government and the constitutent units of North Eastern Council have come to rely upon its counsel and recommendations in all matters relating to socio-economic development of the region. Starting with a modest outlay of Rs. 28.00 lakhs in 1973, the Council's activities have rapidly expanded, and, today, with an annual plan allocation of Rs. 80.00 crores, cover a wide spectrum spanning almost all fields of economic activity, be it development of agriculture, minerals, water, power resources, transportation network or manpower utilization. Indeed the Council stands out in the country as a shining example of how an institution has grown in response to the needs of economic development of the region and its people, and the way it has enhanced its usefulness by helping the process of economic development in every possible way.

ACCELERATED DEVELOPMENT

With the passage of time the Council has gained experience and is entering into newer areas of economic development in a bid to bring about rapid and accelerated development given to it. Mention may be made of the recent decision of the Council, to take up 13 watershed management schemes, with associated programmes, for soil conservation and improvement and development of rich forest resources of the region including agro-forestry and social forestry. These newly introduced programmes aim at maintenance of ecological balance while making optimal use of land. Similarly, in regard to development of industry and energy in the region, recent efforts of North Eastern Council in establishment of four mini-cement plants, construction of roads of economic importance and tapping of non-coventional and renewable resources of energy represent a bold response to the continually changing and dynamically developing situation as the process of development has been unfolding itself, and making its impact felt over various parts of the region.

MAIN THRUST

While the main thrust of the Council's policies and programmes, has been to help the rapid and balanced development of the region, through programmes of regional importance concerning all or more than one State/Union Territory, it has also supplemented the efforts which the constitutent units are making, through their own plans for development of their respective areas. by rendering them such balancing and infrastructural support as they needed. It has also stimulated, and, wherever necessary, supplemented the programmes, of the Central Ministries for development of the region. In short, for development North Eastern Council has acted as a very powerful catalyst of the region over the last decade.

LONG, LONG WAY TO GO

North Eastern Council's achievements have, no doubt been impressive so far, but the tasks which still lie ahead continue to be difficult and challenging Despite all the progress that has been made over the last ten years, the north-eastern region still continues to be one of the lesser developed areas in the country. Though a small dent has been made in removing infrastructural dificiencies, the region has still to go a long way before the inadequacies of road and rail network can be said to have been overcome to a significant extent. Similarly, only a beginning has been made in development of the vast water, power, forest, and mineral resources of the region. Besides making continuous and sustained efforts in these areas in the years to come, the Council will have to address itself to newer areas, adapting its programmes to the fast changing development scenario in the region, such as human resource development and introduction of new and appropriate technologies, so that the economic development of the region is accelerated. As the development of the region proceeds it will be necessary to ensure that the people participate in the development and share in its benefit in full measure.

4
HYDRO-POWER POTENTIALITIES

by
S. N. Phukan

Of the world's entire water resources, 97 percent goes to form the oceans fit only for navigation, 2 percent is lost in the frozen and locked up ice-caps and only one per cent is available for multiple use of the human race. The availability of fresh water in abundance is, therefore, a unique gift of nature, too scarce to be wasted, much too precious to be neglected.

The metrological, topographical and hydrological phenomena combine to make the North Eastern Region (NER) store house of fantastic hydro-electric potential, not only in the country, but also in the world. Much is spoken about these resources, although very little has so far been done. It may be said without fear of contradiction that the greatest natural resource of this remote region is not oil or tea, but water. The region is blessed with two unique river basins, the larger Brahmaputra basin and the smaller Barak basin, both of which can be developed to bestow benefits to the entire country. Of the various benefits which the planned development of these river basins can bring, hydro-electric power generation is certainly the most attractive. With the sharply increasing cost and rapidly decreasing reserves of oil and coal, now in use for power generation, men have begun a hectic search for alternative sources of energy. There can be no better alternative than the available hydro resources, ever replenished by nature, devoid of pollution and unaffected by inflation.

A systematic map study of the hydro-resources of the river systems was made only in the late fifties of this century by the Central Water and Power Commission. By no means exact, this estimate established the possibility or generating about 14 million kilowatts of hydro-power from the rivers of the North Eastern Region. Subsequent studies, made with more recent and better maps, coupled with field investigation have revealed even higher potential. While there may be some variations in these estimated figures, the river system of the region without doubt offers the highest hydro protential in the country in a single region. A basin and tributary-wise examination will unfold the picture of this mostly untapped resources fully.

BRAHMAPUTRA BASIN

The first tributary of the Brahmaputra valley to get the attention of water power engineers is the Umtru river where its cascading rapids were harnessed to provide a tiny power station in July 1957, with only 8.4 megawatt capacity. Ever since that 9th July 1957, this power house has been a steady and firm source of electricity for the region. It must have paid for its cost of two crores of rupees many times over !

While, the Umtru powerhouse was planned and executed as an isolated station, its commissioning planted the seed for conceiving an integrated plan to tap the virgin resources of the entire valley for optimum utilisation. As a result, six more power stations were planned on what is now known as the Umiam-Umtru-Khri valley, in various stages, with a total potential of 400 megawatts. Out of these six, three have since been commissioned progressively with an insstallation of 144 megawatts, beside Umtru with an installation of 11.2 MW after addition of one unit in 1968.

KOPILI—MOST PROMISING SCHEME

Assam Electricity Board's proposal to develop 150 megawatts on the Kopili river, a major south bank tributary of Brahmaputra, received Centre's clearance in 1974-75. The project is now under construction by the North Eastern Electric

Power Corporation. By far the most promising hydro-scheme of this Valley it has a potential for enlarging its scope to a 400 megawatt station with little extra effort. Two other hydel stations planned on the downstream o this river with a potential of 133 MW is now under investigation by the Assam Electricity Board. Kopili Valley when fully tapped can yield 533 megawatts of power.

Assam Electricity Board has started construction work on the 100 MW Lower Borpani hydro-electric project from November 1979. Two other projects on the Borpani river are now under investigation with a potential for installation of 120 MW, th total potential of the valley being 220 MW.

The Board has also completed the investigation for a hydro scheme on the Killing river, before its emergence on to the plains with a proposed installation of 150 MW. This project has not, however, been pursued seriously because of some interstate and submergence problems.

The Centre has recently issued technical clearance to the 105 MW hydro-electric project on the Doyang river in Nagaland. Work on this project can start as soon as the financial resources are tied up.

On the north bank of Brahmaputra, the Central Water Commission has finalised a project report for developing 600 MW on the Kameng river, after several years of detailed investigations.

The North Eastern Electric Power Corporation has undertaken investigation for a 500 MW hydro-power scheme on Ranganadi, on 80 MW scheme on Pappu and a 400 MW scheme at Damwe on the Lohit river basin.

BRAHMAPUTRA TRIBUTARIES

The total potential of the tributaries of the Brahmaputra described so far, and under various stages of investigation, including the four stations since commissioned comes to nearly 3000 MW. About 50 crores of rupees have been spent on the power stations already commissioned with an installation of 125 megawatts. Although, any cost estimates made now, are bound to uudergo changes because of the time frame in the construction of these projects, the estimated cost to tap the balance 2875 MW of power, from the identified projects will run into about 2000 to 2400 crores of rupees, based no current prices. No doubt it is a great deal of money, but it is worth the expenditure and effort to generate over 10,000 million units of electricity. Incidentally it would effect an annual saving of 3 million tonnes of oil or nearly 5 million tonnes of coal. depending on the fuel used, which would otherwise be consumed to generate an equivalent quantum of power.

While on the subject, it will be pertinent to mention that inspite of the many uninformed criticism levelled against the Assam State Electricity Board for developing the Umiam-Umtru hydel project, these power stations have proved beyond any doubt the economy and reliability of the hydro-power system. But for the steady and uninterrupted supply of electricity from these hydro-stations, the northeastern region, including Assam, would have kept company with the notoriety of power cuts and load sheddings of West Bengai and Bihar. In no year, since the commissioning and loading of these power stations has the annual generation been below the rated and design values for the system.

The three million kilowatts of power that we can possibly tap from all the tributaries of Brahamputra, described so far, appear to be chickenfeed, when we turn our attention to the possibilities of Subansiri and Dihang, the two most powerful rivers, flowing into the Brahmaputra valley.

Subansiri, named so for the occurrence of gold in the river, possesses an even more valuable asset in its capacity to generate electric power. A proposal, based on which the investigations were being conducted by the Brhmaputra Flood Control Commission, provided for a 210 metre high rockfill dam on the river, creating a reservoir to store over 6 million acrefeet of water, most of which would be passed through an underground powerhouse turning 9 huge hydro-turbines capable of generating 1800 megawatts of electric power. Until we consider Dihang, this will be the largest hydro power station in the country.

POWER PROJECT THAT TAKES THE CAKE

The most promising yet the most difficult hydro-electric project of the basin is aptly located on the Dihang, the main river channel of Brahmaputra. By any standard of power projects, this one will take the cake ! A 240-metre high rockfill dam, some 20 kilometres upstream of Passighat will create one of the biggest man-made lakes to store a fantastic 20 million acrefeet of water, with a surface area of 350 square kilometers. It is proposed to have a power house with 15 giant generators of 500 megawatts each, which will break all records.

The estimated cost of these two gigantic hydel projects will be, between 8000 to 9000 crores of rupees. But the generation of 50,000 million units of electricity a year will earn for them a handsome gross return of 2500 to 3000 crores of rupees a year, almost 5 to 6 times the present annual value of oil produced in the Assam fields. Nowhere in India, a hydro-electric project of the size and magnitude of Dihang has been contemplated nor is it possible to find any other site like this. A power station of this staggering capacity, can increase the presently installed electric power of the whole country by as much as thirty per cent in one shot.

TWO GIGANTIC PROJECT

Subansiri and Dihaug projects can be undertaken only after the most careful and intensive field investigations and detailed and painstaking analysis of various data requiring the services of technologists of all connected disciplines A dynamic and powerful multidisciplinary organisation with the best of talents will be called for even from the planning stage. Recently, the Government of India have constituted the Brahmaputra Board for the development of water resources of he Brahmaputra and Barak basins The investigations of Subansiri and Dihang now stand transferred to this Board. It is hoped, that the Board would be able to expedite the investigations and plan for these projects on very sound technical basis.

Such projects will perforce need the use of the most advanced and sophisticated technology in design and construction. We must not feel shy to utilise the experience of similiar construction elsewhere in the world, like the 300 meter high Nurek dam built in the USSR and the 265 metre high Grijaiva dam in Mexico now nearing completion.

Besides the technical problems, such projects will also involve environmental and human problems of resettlement. Although not very heavily populated, the reservoir areas consist of habitation and cultivated lands of tribal people of Arunachal. The affected people will have to be benefited in all respects from such projects, although they may have to undergo temporary inconveniences. Examples of various benefits showered on affected people by way of better housing, provision of irrigated cultivable land and employment in small industries set up in the area can be found from such big projects taken up elsewhere in the world like Latin America and Canada.

Let us now have a look at the Barak river system which originates in the Manipur hills and joins the Brahmaputra in Bangladesh.

BARAK RIVER SYSTEM

The Barak river has been under investigation for nearly 20 years for controlling the floods in the Cachar valley. The Central Water Commission has now finalised a project report to construct a 175 meter high dam near Tipaimukh with a proposed power station with an installation of 1500 MW. Possibility of providing a 100 MW hydro scheme on the Tuivai, a tributary of Barak, has been identified.

The Dhameswari river in Mizoram has been taken up for investigations by the National Hydro Electric Power Corporation. It is proposed to install 80 MW of power in this project.

Map studies reveal the possibility of generating hydropower combined with irrigation schemes from the north flowing tributaries of Barak, such as Longai, Singla, Rukni, Sonai which originate in Mizoram to an extent of about 100 MW.

The Loktak hydro-electric project with a capacity of 105 MW is expected to be commissioned by December, 1982. Although, this project utilises the water from the Loktak lake, fed by the Imphal river, the tailrace water will pass on to the Barak basin through the powerhouse. A downstream 2nd stage development of the Loktak with an installed capacity of 100 MW has been planned.

Assam Electricity Board has carried out field reconnaissance and map studies of the Kynshi river in the Khasi Hills. Originating near the Nongstoin ridge, this river cascades down through steep falls, allowing utilisation of nearly 1600 metres of head in two power stations where upto 600 MW can be installed. The project does not involve any appreciable submergence and the geological features are very favourable.

The Umngi river, also Khasi Hills, offers possibility of generating 100 MW in its lower reaches. However, field reconnaissance revealed considerable submergence of cultivable land, for which the detailed investigations for the project were not taken up.

Meghalaya Electricy Board is now investigating the potential of the Myntudu river near Leska in Jaintia Hills, where it is possible to instal 75 MW in two power stations.

It will be seen that identified and projected under investigation in the Barak valley may provide installation of 2760 MW. Together with the identified projects in the main Brahmaputra basin, the hydro potential of the basins in the North-Eastern region comes to over 15 million KW. The potentials of Noadihing, Dibong and Lohit are yet to be fully assessed. It may therefore be possible to provide nearly 20 million KW from the Brahmaputra and Barak river systems in the North Eastern Region

PROSPERITY THROUGH POWER

Much of the economic difficulties of our country has been rightly attributed to the continued shortage of power, restricting optimum production in every field, be it industry or agriculture. It is an acknowledged fact, that availability of cheap and abundant electricity is as much responsible for the spectacular increase in agricultural productivity in the United States, as the availability of improved varieties of seeds and fertilizers. Nearer home, Punjab proves the point with their prosperity by the extensive use of electricity in irrigation.

Arguments that hydro-power generation is required to be balanced with proportionate generation from thermal stations is not corroborated by facts. While it may be true that thermal generation should be balanced with proportionate generation from hydro or pumped storage stations, it is not true the other way round. Countries like Canada, Sweden, Norway meet 75 to 99 per cent of their electricity demand from hydro sources. A Hydro power generator produced nearly 88 per cent of the water's potential as electricity. Whereas a coal or soil fired generator can cover no more than 30 per cent of the inherent energy of the fuel. Development of hydro power resources, therefore, call for the highest attention of the policy makers.

IDEAL CONDITIONS FOR POWER GENERATION

Before I conclude, I must make a mention of one other potential hydro-source of the Brahmaputra, even though it is only of an academic interest upto now. The ideal condition for generating hydro-power. is a great drop for a large volume of water in the shortest possible distance. Nowhere can we find a more ideal condition like this than the hairpin bend of the Tsangpo around the Namcha Barwa gorge. The two limbs of the bend are divided by a distance of 50 kilometers and a fall of 10,000 feet. A 50 kilometre long tunnel can bring the water from an elevation of 11,000 feet to power house at an elevation of 1000 feet, to produce 20 to 30 million kilowatts of power. But then, it will need the cooperation and agreement of two countries, besides the ingenuity to solve the various technical challenges not yet faced anywhere. Upto now, it is only a dream for all imaginative water power engineers.

RALL-CUM-ROAD BRIDGE NEAR GAUHATI

The Committee of Ministers for Economic Development of North East, Government of India, at a meeting has unanimously resolved that there should be a combined project for a rail-cum-road bridge with the connecting rail link on the south bank between Pancharatna and Gauhati which would open up the backward areas of Garo Hills and Goalpara District. Conveying this information in a letter to the Chairman of North Eastern Council, the Union Minister of Home Affairs has said that action for preparation of model studies, framing of estimates and obtaining necessary sanctions would be taken early.

5
AGRICULTURE AND ALLIED SECTORS

by
D.N. Borthakur

The North Eastern Region comprising of five states, viz. Assam, Manipur, Meghalaya, Nagaland and Tripura and two union territories, Arunachal Pradesh and Mizoram has a total geographical area of a little over 25.5 million hectares inhabited by a population of over 20 million people. Nearly 90 per cent of the population lives in the villages. Agriculture, in the real sense, is the primary occupation of the people of the region as over 60 per cent of the population are cultivators, 9.28 per cent are agricultural labourers, while nearly 8 per cent of the population depend on livestock, fishery, forestry, plantation and orchards, etc.

The North Eastern Region again presents a unique geographical area in the sense that there is a wide variation in the altitude ranging from nearly 100 m to over 400 m. The climate and so also the temperature range from tropical plains to temperate hills. The region is well-known for its high rainfall combined with very high humidity. All these factors affect agriculture of the region.

DIFFICULTIES

For historical reasons, this region has remained as a backward area and as such, agriculture of the region has also remained behind the main stream of the country. The net sown area in the region is 3.5 million hectares out of which

Assam alone has 2.6 million hectares. Gross cropped area is about 4 lakh hectares which is about 22 per cent of the net area cultivated. The size of operational holding is also very small being on an average within the range of 0.5 to 2 hectares. Consumption of plant nutrients per gross cropped area is also very low ranging between 3 kg. per ha. in Assam to about 12 kg. per ha in Manipur. There are specific problems which are physical or infrastructural while there are other problems that can be grouped under technical and management. Some of these major problems are transport and communication, marketing, land tenure, un-scientific land use, dearth of technical man-power, post-harvest facilities, problems of inputs supply due to difficult terrain and inaccessibility of areas, lack of adequate extension support, lack of in-service training to extension personnel, inadequate irrigated areas, low utilization of technology including implements, acidic soil, high rainfall and humidity, low temperature during winter, undulating topography, sloppy hills and varying altitudes, etc.

In addition to above, there are four special problems of the region. These are the problems of soil and water conservation including the practice of shifting cultivation, the problem of citrus decline, socio-economic constraints and the problem of floods in the plains.

POTENTIALITIES

In spite of peculiar problems mentioned above, the potentialities of agriculture in the whole region is very vast. Besides, the food crops and fibre crops potentialities exist for growing a large number of other economic crops and plants. Rice, maize, wheat and ragi are important cereals while tuber crops, such as tapioca, yams and sweet potato, oil seeds, primarily mustard and sesaems, sugarcane, jute, mesta, ramie, cotton, pulse crops such as blackgram, greengram, pea, soyabean, arhar and lentil are all important crops of the region. Besides vegetables, all kinds of horticultural crops such as citrus, banana, pineapple, peach, plum, pears, apples, apricot and walnut, etc. can be successfully grown in different altitudes. Among the spice crops, ginger, turmeric, black pepper, cardamom and cinnamon hold great promise for development.

There are many indigenous crops containing aromatic, medicinal and pesticidal properties, etc. in the region. Similarly, this region is also noted for the presence of various kinds of orchids. It is the original home of many other crops and plants such as mandarin organs. The genetic variability of the various crops, existing in the region, can be of immense value for improvement of crops all over the world.

The importance of plantation crops such as tea, coffee, rubber are already well-known. Similarly, forest trees of economic importance including fodder and fuel trees as well as canes and bamboos are of great relevance of the region.

Prospects of animal husbandry is very good, specially in the hilly region. Pig is by far the most important livestock for the hilly areas. This region is again endowed with rare species such as mithun, yak and wild boar. The Himalayan sheep of Arunachal Pradesh is also a very important species of livestock. In aquaculture, indigenous fishes like Masheer and trout are considered to be very important.

AGRO-BASED INDUSTRIES

Besides the potentialities mentioned above, there is immense scope for development of agro-based industries in the region. The agro-industrial potentialities of some crops have already been exploited. These include tea, jute, sugarcane, pineapple, orange and some other fruits Recently, citronella, an aromatic crop, has emerged as an important crop with industrial potentiality. Similarly coffee and rubber are two other crops, which have shown potentiality of large scale cultivation.

An important group of crops awaiting proper exploitation is the spice crops. These include ginger, turmeric, black pepper, large cardamom and cinnamon. Southern states presently export most of the black pepper and turmeric. Both these crops grow here extremely well. It is of interest to mention here that the higher cucumin content of turmeric variety grown in Jowai District of Meghalaya is higher by one per cent than that of the varieties grown in the South. Similarly, north eastern region can become the primary source of cinnamon also.

Yams, tapioca, sweet potato and maize are widely grown in the region. These plants are important sources of carbohydrate and starch and hence can be utilized for starch powder and as ingredient of livestock feed. Soyabean which grows extremely well in the region needs to be mentioned here. Soyabean is not only the source of oil but because of the high protein content, it can also be utilized as an ingredient of livestock feed. Livestock feed industry thus has a great scope.

A hitherto underutilised plant is ramie. This crop has a great prospect of being grown, more specially in Assam as a source of blendable fibre for the polyeter complex proposed to be established there. Orchids growing wild in the region have immense potentiality in the export market.

Agro-waste utilisation is another area that deserves consideration. About 2 per cent of arecanut produced in the country, come from this region. Process for making highly density hard boards from arecanut wastes has been developed by Forest Research Institute, Dehradun. The Regional Research Laboratory at Jorhat has reported utilization of paddy husk for production of molecular sieves, brick and cement. Similarly jute, stick, bagasee, paddy straw and decaffinated tea waste have been utilized for making paper boards and building materials. Rice straw, paddy husk, jute stick and bagasee have also been used for production of an industrial chemical known as furfural. Production of caffeine from tea waste is already well-known. Ethanol and its derivatives can be produced from sugarcane and tapioca.

The oil from Tazpatta (Cinnamomum tarnata) available in Meghalaya in large quantities, contains 70-80 per cent eugenol suitable for preparation of perfumary chemicals.

A large number of citrus species are available in the region. Analysis of juice volume and citric acid content of these species has indicated that some species contain very high percentage of citric acid and hence opens up potentiality for production of this important chemical. Prospects of production of enzymes such as bromelin from pineapple waste and papain from papaya also need to be exploited.

Weeds like water hyacinth have been successfuly utilized for production of biomas as a source of energy as well as for making paper boards. Studies are required for hydro-carbon yielding plants.

Sericulture is already an established small industry of the region since all four varieties of silk worm, namely eri, muga, mulberry and oak tassar can be successfully raised.

There are several other medicinal, aromatic and insecticide yielding plants that await proper exploration. These include, Coptis teeta (mishimi teeta), lemon grass, Pyrathrum sap, etc.

The forest wealth of this region is very well-known. Proper exploitation and regeneration and management of the forest wealth including bamboos, canes, etc. can really provide maximum employment generation and land based enterprises.

INSTITUTIONAL SETUP FOR DEVELOPMENT

The institutional setup for development of agriculture in the region has come up in an appropriate manner only during the last decade. During this period, the development departments of the states and union territories have also been strengthened adequately. The Assam Agricultural University, with its teaching, research and extension wings, has been helping in solving the problems of agriculture primarily of the state. Two more agricultural colleges, one in Nagaland and the other in Manipur has been started recently. In addition to the above the two major infrastructural development are the establishment of the North Eastern Council and the involvement of Indian Council of Agricultural Research in a major way in the development of agriculture of the ragion.

ROLE OF ICAR

The Indian Council of Agricultural Research has sanctioned a large number of research schemes to the Assam Agricultural University besides providing funds for development of the University as a whole including its teaching and extension wings. There are four other projects of the ICAR in the State of Assam. These are the Central Plantation Crop Research Institute at Kahikuchi, Gauhati, a centre on Ramie Research at Sorbhog under the Agricultural Reseach Institute; the units of Co-ordinated Research projects in composite fish culture and air breathing fishes at Gauhati, and the Regional Centre of National Bureau of Land Use and Soil Survey at Jorhat. The ICAR has also a scheme on Human Resource Development for providing financial assistance to students for undergoing both under-graduate and post-graduate studies. In addition, the ICAR has a collaboration with the North Eastern Council to provide seats for students of this region in various agricultural universities of the country. However, the most important contribution of the ICAR is the establishment in 1975 of a full-fledged research institute, called the ICAR Research Complex for North Eastern Hills Region with its main centre in Meghalaya and strong research centres in Manipur, Nagaland, Tripura, Mizoram, Arunachal Pradesh and Sikkim. The Institute has in its fold responsiblities of research in all the fields of agriculture, animal sciences, fisheries, soil and water conservation, agricultural engineering and also agro-forestry. The Institute also has four Krishi Vigyan Kendras and A Trainers' Training Centre attached to it. This institute during its short span of existence in the region, has been able to recommend/develop suitable varieties and technology for increasing production of field crops, horticultural crops, animals and fishes in the region. The Institute has been able to study in detail and find out the causes of a major problem like citrus decline and has now been involved in rejuvenation of aspects of shifting cultivation has been studied by the Institute and it is in the process of advocating alternatings of the Institute have now started percolating down to the fields of the farmers through its national demonstrations, lab-to-land programmes, training in the Krishi Vigyan Kendras of the institute, organisation of training at various levels including extension officers, farmers, etc. and through collaborations with the NEC in its development projects.

ROLE OF NORTH EASTERN COUNCIL

The NEC has played a very major role since its establishment in (i) the development of infrastructure such as seed farms/orchards, irrigation, removal of transport bottleneck, (ii) transfer of technology, (iii) tackling problems of marketing and (iv) in training of man-power. The budget allotment provided by NEC for agriculture and allied sectors are shown in Tables 1 and 2.

Table 1

Allotment of Funds in North Eastern Council Budget for Agriculture and Allied Services

(in lakh rupees)

1974-75 to 1977-78	Interim 6th Plan period 197 -79 to 1982-83	6th Plan 1980-81 to 1984-85
1329.56	2400.52	3000.38

Table 2

Sectorwise Allotment of Funds in North Eastern Council Budget —During 6th Plan Period

(in lakh rupees)

Head	Allotment		
	Continuing Scheme	New Scheme	Total
1	2	3	4
Agriculture	617 00	55.00	672 00
Horticulture	1007.87	287.00	1294.87
An mal Husbandry	150.79	228.53	379.32
Fisheries	29.00	127.00	156.00
Plantation Crops	115.75	382.44	499.19
	1920.41	1079.97	3000.38

PRODUCTION OF PLANTING MATERIALS

Since, availability of recommended planting materials of various crops is a bottleneck, North Eastern Council has taken steps for establishment of seed farms for production of foundation seeds. Such farms have been established separately for field crops and potatoes. Similarly, progeny orchards and nurseries have been established to meet the requirement of the planting materials of horticultural crops and vegetable seeds.

In order to improve the quality of local livestock North Eastern Council has set up farms for breeding superior livestocks, such as cattle, poultry, duck and sheep. Fodder seed production farms have also been set up to provide for the planting materials.

Availability of fish seed is another area which requires attention. North Eastern Council has, therefore, taken steps to provide for fish seed farms for different altitude ranges. Similarly, nurseries have been established for providing planting materials of plantation crops, more specifically of coffee and rubber.

SHIFTING CULTIVATION

Shifting cultivation is a major problem of this area. North Eastern Council in the Fifth Five Year Plan took up eight pilot projects for settlement of jhumies and 5295 families were settled under the programme after developing an area of 11300 ha. During the Sixth Five Year Plan, North Eastern Council has decided to take pilot projects on a few priority sub-water sheds in order to tackle the problem of shifting cultivation on the basis of proper land use and development of farming system. In addition to this, planning and management and water sheds have been incorporated in the programme of North Eastern Council during the Sixth Five Year Plan. In such water shed planning, emphasis will be laid on efficient land use on the basis of research findings of the ICAR Research Complex at Shillong incorporating basic concepts of agro-forestry, horti-pastoral and silvi-pastoral systems as well as food crop farming.

MAN-POWER DEVELOPMENT

The dearth of technical man-power is one of the major constraints for development of the region. The dearth of man-power is acute not only at the professional level but also at the para-professional level. North Eastern Council has financed the

Assam Agricultural University to reserve seats for the students of the States and Union territories of the region other than Assam in the constitutent colleges of the University. Further with the assistance of ICAR North Eastern Council reserves a large number of seats for Bachelors, Masters degree courses as well as Ph.D. programme in various fields of agriculture and related subjects and scholarships are provided to the students on the recommendation of the state governments. In this programme North Eastern Council has assisted more than 900 students for higher studies.

In addition to the above, short-term specialised training in various fields, like soil conservation, water shed management, seed production, cultivation of field and fodder crops plant protection, plantation crops, swine husbandry and fisheries have also been sponsord. The Council has in its programme now the establishment of a Soil Conservation Staff Training Centre as well as a Regional Institute for Science and Technology to augment man-power development. It may be mentioned in this connection that funds provided for man-power development are in addition to the amount earmarked for agriculture and allied sectors.

SPECIFIED PROGRAMMES

During the Sixth plan period, the North Eastern Council has proposed a number of specified programmes for augmenting production. Mention may be made of pilot demonstrations for rejuvenation of citrus orchards in the north eastern region. This programme is based on the findings of research already done on the subject by ICAR Research Complex for North Eastern Hills Region. Similarly, a regional centre for training and production of mushroom has also been proposed. This is also based on the technology developed by the ICAR Research complex. Another such programme that deserves mention is the conservation and multiplication of the orchids of the north-eastern region. This collaborative programme has been drawn up with Botanical Survey of India and the ICAR Reseaich Complex. A scheme for establishment of a regional centre for production of bio-fertilizers has also been sanctioned. It will be operated by Assam Agricultural University.

DEVELOPMENT OF INFRASTRUCTURE

For development of irrigation potentiality, ground water survey and development has been included as an important programme under North Eastern Council. Similarly, improvement of transport and communication of the region and development of hydel power potentiality of the region are sectors of development which will directly benefit production programme of agriculture and allied sectors. One major step towards enhancing agricultural production is the proposed programme of North Eastern Council to establish Regional Agricultural Marketing Corporation. Lack of marketing facilities presently has not been able to provide the required idncentives for growing horticultural crops of which the region has vast potentiality.

OTHER PROJECTS

The North Eastern Council has also sponsored several schemes to be operated by the Assam Agricultural University, North Eastern Hills University as well as Gauhati University on various aspects. Besides providing facilities for augmenting training in Assam Agricultural University, a special scheme for training of in-service personnel has been sanctioned. A rescarch project on economic use of water hyacinth has been approved for the Gauhati University. In addition to this, various other surveys including soil survey with the help of ICAR are being continued by the North Eastern Council for development of agriculture in the region.

It appears that the scope for increasing agricultural production, development of agro-based industries, generation of gainful employment through land and water-based enterprises and improving the economic conditions of the people of the region is rather vast. A good beginning has been made and if the programme already taken up by the various agencies can be carried out effectively and spread amongst the masses, not only can ecology of the region be preserved and natural endowment be harnessed and sustained but the whole region can be developed into one of the richest areas in the country in the field of agriculture.

6

MANPOWER DEVELOPMENT

by

R.N. Tandon

Manpower planning has assumed a significant role for carrying out the programme of economic development all over the world. Economic planning and Manpower Planning are two inseparable parts and are complementary to each other. It has been realised that economic development cannot take place without proper planning for manpower development, as suitably technically qualified people are required to carry out these programmes. The inadequacy of technically qualified people has been one of the most important factors for the backwardness of the north eastern region. The programmes of development envisaged in the state and Union Territory plans, require various categories of trained personnel-scientific, technological, managerial, etc. to implement such programmes. There is an over all dearth of trained people in the fields of agriculture, horticulture, fisheries, animal husbandry, sericulture, industries, medicine, irrigation, power, mineral exploitation, etc. The Governments of stases and Union territories of this region are quite alive to this lacuna. Over the plans, efforts are being made by them to bridge this gap.

The North Eastern Council realising the inadequacy of technically trained people in the region took steps to correct this imbalance. The Planning Commission approved an outlay of Rs. 18.45 crores for manpower development in the NEC's Sixth Plan. For the year 1981-82 the approved outlay was Rs.

2.55 crores and approved outlay for Annual Plan 1982-83 is Rs. 5.29 crores.

DEVELOPMENT OF MANPOWER

The Council has been making efforts for the development of manpower both technical and non-technical in four ways, viz., (*a*) sponsoring of personnel from this region for under-graduate and post-graduate studies; (*b*) sponsoring candidates for short duration specialised courses; (*c*) setting up of new institutions in the region and finally; (*d*) by expansion or strengthening of the institutes already existing in the region.

As is already known that agriculture is the main support of the people of the region. NEC started training people in agriculture and allied subjects as a first step. A scheme was formulated in 1975 under which the North Eastern Council started sponsoring candidates from this region for under-graduate and postgraduate studies in the fields of agriculture and allied subjects in the different universities of the country. The Council also gave scholarships/stipends to the candidates selected to pursue these courses. The scheme has been a big success. The tempo of this scheme is being gradually increased and it will be continued till it is felt that we have sufficient number of people trained in these fields.

SPECIALISED TRAINING

Apart from sponsoring candidates for under-graduate and post-graduate courses, the Council also sponsors in service candidates for various specialised short term training programmes which are being conducted by well recognised institutes/universities of the country in various fields like soil conservation, watershed management, seed production, cultivation of field and fruit crops, plant protection, plantation, swine husbandry, fisheries, etc. The Council has so far identified 35 such special short term training programmes.

The North Eastern Cuncil with a view to increasing the number of seats in the Assam Agricultural University offered financial assistance to it to meet its capital expenditure for adding hostels, laboratories and equipment. The Assam

Agricultural University is offering North Eastern Council additional 35 seates for the B. Sc. course and30 seats for B.V. Sc. courses every year, for the participants of the states other than Assam.

It was observed that the region had only one Agricultural University in Assam with limited number of seats. Another College of Agriculture was set up in Nagaland a few years back under auspices of the North Eastern Hill University with an annual intake of 50 students. Recently Government of Manipur has also established an Agricultural College in Imphal with an annual intake of 40 candidates. Besides, NEC has helped in the expansion of the school of veterinary sciences and animal husbandry at Ghungoor, and Fisheries Training Institute at Joysagar.

The Council has a scheme to augment the faculty of the Assam Agricultural University to enable it to have visiting professors *i.e.* Professors of repute, whose services could be obtained by the university for short periods. The Council has another scheme under which "Refreshers Training Courses" are organised in agriculture, animal husbandry and veterinary sciences by the Assam Agricultural University at their campuses at Jorhat and Khanapara for inservice candidates of the region. These courses are aimed at familiarising the personnel with the recent advances and modern techniques in their fields. The Council also organises special training programmes for development of fishery in her North Eastern Region in collaboration with the Central Institute of Fisheries, Bombay.

SIGNIFICANT CONTRIBUTION

The Council has also made significant contribution in the field of health and medical sciences. It may be mentioned that the doctors-population ratio appropriate for the rest of the country as a whole may not be applicable to the region. It is possible to visualise a surplus in the country as a whole and an acute shortage in the north eastern region at the same time or vice-versa. There are obvious limitations on the mobility of these persons when this region is concerned and the constraint arises not only from the unwillingness of outside personnel to work in this area but also from the natural and legitimate expectations of the people of this region to find their own qualified personnel. Keeping in view this limitation, the North Eastern Council financed setting up of a Regional Medical College in Manipur. Its benefits are shared by all the constituent states except Assam. Assam has already three Medical colleges. Similarly for the training of nurses NEC started and funded a Regional Graduate College of Nursing at Gauhati where graduate nurses are being trained for the entire region. To overcome the shortage of qualified pharmacists in the region, the Council has set up a Regional Institute of Pharmacy at Agartala with an annual intake of 50. Besides, students for B.Sc. and M.Sc. pharmacy are being sponsored to recognised universities for taking these courses. The Sixth Plan of the North Eastern Council provides for starting a B. Pharma course in Assam Medical College, Dibrugarh. A Dental Wing has also been started at Gauhati Medical College for a year's B.D.S. Course.

To meet the shortage of Engineers, NEC is assisting the Tripura Engineering College to increase the intake of students from 60 to 120. The Assam Engineering Institute which runs a diploma course in Chemical Engineering is being assisted to increase its annual intake from 35 to 50. The Council is also contemplating to strengthen existing Institute of the Region, to provide specialised training in fields like Agricultural Engineering, Chemical Engineering, Food Technology, Electronics and Telecommunications, Petroleum Technology, etc.

It may be significant to point out that the North Eastern Council is working on the setting up of an Institute of Science and Technology at Itanagar, Arunachal Pradesh.

INDUSTRIAL TRAINING

For the development of industries in the region, Council had in the past conducted courses on small scale industries in collaboration with the Small Industry Extension Running Institute, Gauhati. It is proposed to have these courses in future years too. NEC is running a special one year course for training of drillers in collaboration with NEEPCO. In the field of sericulture, the Council has taken steps to increase the intake of students in the Sericulture Training Institute and also sponsor candidates for post-graduate diploma and degree courses in sericulture in the Sericulture Institute at Ranchi, Mysore and Berhampur. Besides, the North Fastern Council is organising several other short term training programmes of two to three weeks, duration in collaboration with the Indian Institutes of Management, Ahmedabad and Calcutta, Central Institute of Road Transport, Poona, All India Management and Training, New Delhi, Institute of Secretariat Management and Training, New Delhi to train people of this region in modern system of planning and control in different fields.

To encourage more and more students to go in for specialised engineering courses, the North Eastern Council has a scheme under which stipends are given to students who of their own get admission in specialised branches of engineering. The Council gives stipends to students who are pursuing studies in Management courses in reputed institutes of the country.

Although the task of manpower development is collosal, it is hoped that the efforts which are being put in by the North Eastern Council will go a long way in providing technically qualified personnel to man the job in this region.

7

MINERAL DEVELOPMENT

by

Dr. D.K. Ray.

Though only a quarter of the North Eastern Region has been geologically mapped, yet numerous promising mineral deposits have already been located. Even from the meagre geological exploration done so far, the high mineral potential of the region is apparent. The principal mineral resources are those of petroleum-natural as, coal, limestone-dolomite and ceramic and refractory raw materials. Recent surveys have located some deposits of metallic minerals as well,

Mineral development started early in the region but remained restricted to petroleum and coal only till very recent times. Oil fields and linked industries have developed fairly rapidly during the last two decades. Already there are three refineries and two petrochemical complexes. Natural gas is also being used for manufacture of fertiliser at Namrup and generation of power at Namrup and Lakwa.

Mining of coal started in the Makum coalfield quite early. Subsequently regular mining was also done for sometime at Borjan (Nagaland) and Jaipur (Assam). Small cottage-type coal mining was widely prevalent in different areas of Meghalaya (Laitryngew, Bapung, etc.) but currently the North Eastern Coalfields of Coal India Ltd. have their mines in Mekum and Jaipur-Dilli fields only. Cottage-type mining is, however, continuing unabated in Meghalaya, especially in Bapung area of Jaintia Hills.

Though endowed with good limestone deposits, some of which are in close proximity to coal deposits, yet the first cement plant of the region was commissioned in 1966 only at Cherrapunji (Meghalaya). The Second Plant at Bokajan (Assam) became operational in 1976. Together these plants have an installed capacity of about 0.4 million tonnes per year, and the plant at Cherrapunji would soon add 0.12 million tonnes to its capacity. Limestone is being exploited at Komorrah (Meghalaya) for the Chhatak Cement Plant of Bangladesh.

The Sonapahar area of Meghalaya is well-known for the Sillimanite deposits. Though the principal production of Sillimanite refractory comes from this area, the production is declining at present.

Ceramics raw materials, though occurring widely and in promising quantities, have been developed only sporadically for manufacture of insulators, etc.

The chromite deposits of Manipur have been intermittently mined on a small scale and taken out to Orissa for use in ferrochrome factory.

The foregoing briefly summarises the current mineral development activity in the North Eastern Region. This is considered to be rather inadequate vis-a-vis the potentials, but development has been tardy due to a number of reasons which are analysed in this document. The North Eastern Council is endeavouring to accelerate the process of development and expansion of mineral industry in the region through an integrated plan. The activities under this plan have gained momentum during the VI Plan period. The strategy of the same and the programme are discussed in this document.

MINERAL POTENTIALS

The total reserves (all categories) of limestone of cement and higher grades have been estimated at more than 500 million tonnes. Besides those of Mawmuluh and Mawsamai(Meghalaya), Komorrah (Meghalaya) and Dillail Prabat (Assam) which are being exploited for cement manufacture, other good deposits of limestone occur in Siju, Shell-Bholaganj and Lumshang-

Nongkhlieh belts of Meghalaya, Garampani-Umrangso belt of Assam, Tidding area of Arunachal, Nimi and Wazeho areas of Nagaland and Ukhrul Hundung belt of Manipur. Chemical grade limestones occur in Shella-Bholaganj, Lumshang-Nongkhlieh, Nimi, Wazeho and Tidding deposits. Recently, some bands of chemical grade limestone have been reported from the extension areas of Garampani-Umrangso deposits.

The main coalfields are in Assam, Arunachal Pradesh, Meghalaya and Nagaland. Estimates of reserves of all categories vary widely, but the most conservative estimate indicates reserves of about 900 million tonnes. Mining activity under Coal India Ltd. is concentrated in the Makum and Jaipur fields of Assam. Other promising fields are those of West Darranggiri, Siju, Langrin and Bapung (Meghalaya), Namchik-Namphuk (Arunachal), Jaipur-Dilli (Assam) and Borjan (Nagaland).

The oil-fields are mostly in Upper Assam and are operated by the ONGC and the Oil India Ltd. Recently oil-fields have been opened up in Nagaland as well.

For refractories and dolomites the outlook is bright. The reassessment of Sonapahar sillimanite deposits is currently in progress and future prospects are not encouraging. Recently reconnaissance by the Geological Survey has revealed promising Kvanite deposits in Meghalaya, while the Directorate of Geology and Mining of Assam are investigating into the sillimanite deposits of Mikir Hills. Occurrences of fire clay in Garo Hills are already known. The other promising occurrence is that of graphite in Lalpani area of Arunachal. Systematic assessment of the potentials of the recent finds would be available only in the coming years.

Besides the dolomite deposits of Meghalaya, good deposits of dolomite have been reported from Rupa and Menga areas of Arunachal, and both are under active investigation.

Good deposits of clay and glass sand have been studied in Meghalaya, Assam and Tripura. Industrial testing has been done. Recently fairly promising clay deposits have been reported from Rangapahar area of Nagaland. Samples of this clay are being studied.

Banded magnelite hemalite rocks have been reported and

studied in Assam and Nagaland. The deposits are small and potentials are restricted. The Pokhpur magnelite deposit was considered to be of promise because of its nickel content. Studies are in progress. The ophiolite belt of Eastern Nagaland and Mauipur contains numerous pockets of chromite which have been exploited in Manipur. Studies carried out so far have not revealed major deposits. Base metal ores have been reported both from the ophiolite and the metamorphics further east. Intensive studies are in progress.

Base metal sulphides do occur sporadically in Meghalaya and Arunachal. The potentials are not known fully as yet.

Carbonlite complexes of Meghalaya plateau are associated with phosphates and ore earth. Exploration is currently under way.

CONSTRAINTS ON DEVELOPMENT

The constraints which have retarded mineral development in the region are enumerated below :

1. Slow progress of regional resource surveys and inadequate basic documentation.
2. Remoteness and lack of infrastructure.
3. Non-availability of precise information on actually r⁻isable reserves of mineral raw materials, as investigations on the deposits have alredy progressed beyond reconnaissance or preliminary exploration prospecting.
4. Shortage of man-power for mineral exploration and development and
5. Non-availability of data on industrial testing of mineral raw materials.

ROLE OF NORTH EASTERN COUNCIL

The foregoing analysis has been necessary for bringing out the relevance and strategy of NEC's activities and programmes in the domain of mineral exploration and development. The basic objective of all NEC programmes is to ensure integrated and balanced regional development. Such development would depend to a large extent on industries and especially mineral-based industries, if we consider the resource endownents of the north east. It was, therefore, realised that NEC would be required to play a significant role in the following domains for accelerating mineral industry in the region :

1. Acceleration of regional resource assessment for preparation of basic documentation;
2. Acceleration and initiation of programmes for precise estimation of mineral reserves and grades to facilitate exploitation planning;
3. Development of infrastructure;
4. R & D efforts for industrial utilisation of regional mineral raw materials;
5. Techno-economic feasibility studies for mineral industry, and
6. Actual development of pilot-industries to initiate the process of mineral development.

ACHIEVEMENTS AND HIGHLIGHTS

NEC's inception was so close to the beginning of the Fifth Plan period that a thorough assessment of the prevailing development scene and potentials was hardly possible for formulation of plan proposals. However, during the Fifth Plan period the emphasis was on rapid surveys for first approximation resources assessement remote sensing techniques.

However, in the Sixth Plan period the programme underwent a transformation and major elaboration through the inclusion of a major scheme of detailed exploration and proving operations in mineral deposits of promise, development of manpower and infrastructure, a wide range of techno-economic feasibility studies for mineral industry and R & D projects. The remote sensing surveys were also programmed for completion during the Sixth Plan period.

REMOTE SENSING SURVEYS

These surveys commenced during the Fiffth Plan period and are in the final stages now. Under this programme, the National Remote Sensing Agency surveyed the Upper Barak Watershed aıea, Nagaland, Mizoram, Tripura and Brahmaputra Valley. The last phase of the survey, currently in progress is continuing in Lower Barak Watershed area, Arunachal Pradesh and Meghalaya. This programme aims at multi-resource assessment and includes outputs pertaining to land-use, forestry, soil types, geological and geomorphological framework and hydrography.

Under a sister programme aeromagnetic survey was carried out over central and eastern Manipur and the entire Meghalaya including parts of Assam. These surveys provided anomalies which are currently being investigated further by the specialist agencies.

DETAILED MINERAL EXPLORATION AND PROVING

During the Fiffth Plan period the reserves of coal in Mawlong-Shells Coalfied were proved through a detailed investigation under NEF sponsorship. The objective was to prove adequate coal reserves for developing a captive coal-mine for the Mawluh Cherra Cement Plant, which suffers continually due to irregular supply of coal. The reserves and configuration established in course of this investigation indicated that only small scale mining would be possible in this prospect.

During the Sixth Plan period detailed exploration and proving of reserves in eight principal deposts of limestone, coal and basemetal ores have been approved under NEC Plan. Currently detailed exploration and proving of limestone and coal reserves are in Siju (Meghalaya), Bapung Coalfield (Meghalaya), Namchik Coalfield (Arunachal) and Borjan Coalfield (Nagaland). Under the same programme detailed exploration and proving of coal reserves in Dilli-Jeypore Coalfied (Assam) and Langrim Coalfield (Meghalaya) are also proposed to be taken up during 1983-84. Detailed exploration of high-grade limestone in Lumshang (Meghalaya) and base-metal ores in Eastern Manipur-Nagaland are also planned under the programmes. Under a separate scheme the reserves and grades of limestone in Umrangso (N.C. Hills, Assam) have been established and raw material investigation on Lumshang limestone deposit in a pilot segment has also been completed for preparing the basic documentation for the proposed cement and paper grade lime plants respectively.

MANPOWER DEVELOPMENT

Under continuing schemes training is being imparted to diamond core drilliers. Summer course and field training course are continuing for mineral exploration. Operational and management personnel of one cement plant have been trained under another continuing scheme, and the same is envisaged for personnel of the approved cement projects under NEC Plan. Professional staff for the proposed Borjan coalmine is also being developed under a separate scheme.

INFRASTRUCTURE

For opening up access to mineral deposits and remote and inaccessible areas a number of roads of economic importance are under construction. The total outlay earmarked for such roads is more than Rs. 60.00 crores. Besides roads, helipads have been constructed and airlift support is being provided by the NEC for facilitating mineral exploration activities by specialist agencies.

TECHNO-ECONOMIC FEASIBILITY STUDIES

To pave the way for industrial development feasibility studies and project report are sponsored by the North Eastern Council. Studies completed so far include those for cement plant in Jaintia Hills (Meghalaya), Tezu (Arunachal), Wazemoand Nimi (Nagaland) and Umrangso (Assam), pozzolana plants for all the constituent units of the region and for a paper-grade lime plant in Jaintia Hills (Meghalaya). A similar study for a second lime plant, to be located in N.C. Hills, Assam is under consideration.

LARGE AND MEDIUM INDUSTRY

Under the Sixth Plan, the Planning Commission had desired the NEC to set up mini-cement plants in the North Eastern Region to introduce this developming technology considered to be very appropriate for the region. Four plants of capacities ranging from 30 to 200 tpd will be set up under this Programme at an estimated outlay of Rs. 11.00 crores. Construction of the first plant at Tezu (Arunachal) is nearing completion and those at Wazeho (Nagaland) and Hundung (Manipur) will be taken up. The Tezu Plant will have a capacity of 30 tpd and the rest 50 tpd. All the three plants would be of VSK type. The forth plant of 200 tpd capacity will be set up at Umrangso (Assam) and the project documents are now under scrutiny Preparations for setting up a pzozolana plant in Tripura are also quite advanced.

For the existing and upcoming paper mills, which are being set up by the Hindustan Paper Corporation in the North Eastern Region, large quantities of paper grade lime will be required. Currently the plan is to transport this lime from sources in Central India. Considering the limited railway capacity, the Planning Commission desired NEC to explore the possibilities of setting up such lime plants within the North Eastern Region. Two lime plants are thus proposed to be set up, and raw material investigation and location study for the first plant has just been completed.

R & D PROJECTS

Testing of mineral raw materials for ascertaining their suitability for industrial development is a vital pre-requisite. Such endeavours for the north eastern raw materials have been initiated by NEC. Studies completed include those on Didding (Arunachal) and Umrangso (Assam) limestones for cement manufacture and various limestones and clays for making lime pozzolane mixture. Studies are currently in progress for ascertaining the suitability of Lumshang limestone (Meghalaya) for manufacturing paper grade lime, Pokhpur ni-magetite (Nagaland) for nickel extradion and Rangapahar clay (Nagaland) for pottery and sanitaryware. Studies on Umrangso limestone for paper-grade lime making has also been programmed.

Considerable attention is being given to find out ways of better utilisation of the north-eastern coal. High sulpher content of this coal stands in the way of its utilisation in various industries and for power generation. Moreover, the upcoming mini cement plants of the region would require substantial quantities of coke breeze and this is to be brought from West Bengal till regional sources are established. For these purposes two R & D projects for coke making from north eastern coal and fluidised bed combustion of the same are now in progress under NEC sponsorship in the Regional Research Laboratory, Jorhat, with technical collaboration from BHEL.

PERSPECTIVE PLAN

Mineral development has a slow progress. The timespan of five year plans often proves inadequate for comprehensive planning. Hence a longer time-span is necessary for mineral development planning. This plan provides the framework for shorter-term detailed planning and programming.

A long term mineral development plan is, therefore, necessary for the North Eastern Region. A twenty-year plan till 2,000 AD could be conceived but such long term or perspective plan may not be realistic as resource-utilisation patterns are changing fast with technical development. A ten-year plan was, therefore, considered as an acceptable compromise.

Such planning for mineral development in the northeast would of necessity have to be restricted to the two principal mineral raw materials, i.e. limestone and coal. The rest, i.e. clays, refractories and possibly base-metal ores have been excluded from the purview of this attempt, as long term planning for ceramics and refactories is not warranted, and the assessment of multi-metal ore potentials is yet to be done. Though the documentation available for limestone and coal is inadequate for actual development in a number of instances, yet is indicative enough for long term plannning.

A Ten-Year Perspective Plan for manufacturing cement in the North Eastern Region was prepared by the NEC Secretariat in late 1980, and submitted to the Planning Commission. The demand survey preceding the plan formulation exercise revealed that demand for cement in the region would rise to 1.54 million tonnes in 1985 and 2.80 million tonnes in

1990. The perspective plan envisaged additional capacity generation to the extent of 2 64 million tonnes at an estimated outlay of Rs. 269.60 crores. The attendant plan for developing coal mining envisaged raising the coal production capacity to 3.15 million tonnes by 1990 at an estimated outlay of about Rs. 42.00 crores. This plan also included assessment of manpower requirement and schedules for manpower training. The infrastructural developmental plan was also estimated to need another Rs. 72.00 crores.

DEMAND SURVEY

Subsequently, at the request of the Planning Commission the NEC Secretariat conducted a demand survey for coal in the North Eastern Region. In a multi-institutional meeting held in the Council Secretariat the demand figures were finalised at 2.66 million tonnes (1984-85) and 44.1 million tonnes (1989-90). The Bengal-Bihar coal components of this demand were also worked out simultaneously.

These demand projections which were agreed to by the concerned agencies led to advance planning for augmentation of production of coal from the existing mines as well as opening of new mines. The target of production from the lease held areas of NECF has been raised from 1.0 million tonnes to 1.2 million tonnes for 1984-85. Advance planning has also been done to raise the production to 2 23 million tonnes by 1989-90 and 3.78 million tonnes by 2000 AD. While the main production is envisaged from the Makum coalfield, opening of new mines in West Darrangiri coalfield (Meghalaya) and Nemchik coalfield (Arunachal) has also been planned. Detailed exploration in Namchik coalfield is already in progress under the NEC scheme, and the envisaged mine will utilise the data resulting from the NEC sponsored exploration programme.

For the envisaged production for 1989-90, elaborate planning is currently underway for additional exploration and proving operations, so that additional reserves are proved for sustaining the envisaged augmented production. Under two phases ending in 1990 sufficient additional exploration and proving are proposed to be done to establish additional reserves of the order of 88 million tonnes. During the remainder of the Sixth Plan period, NEC sponsorship of the additional exploration programme has been sought and a finalised proposal will soon be submitted to the Planning Commission. For the Seventh Plan period it has been agreed between all concerned agencies that the additional exploration programme will largely be a responsibility of the Coal India Limited though supplementations from other agencies will be considered.

While the development of limestone and coal deposits for exploitation has been planned after consulting all concerned central and state agencies, a similar exercise for refractories and ceramic is long overdue. Since such mineral raw materials may be used for small industries only it is felt that appropriate action could be initiated by State/UT Governments. However, the North Eastern Council would continue to extend assistance to the State/UT Governments in this regard.

A word is due here in respect of petro-chemical industry. While planning is done from the centre, the Noth Eastern Council have been approached for assistance in regard to development of down-stream industries linked to the Bongaigaon Refinery and Petro-chemical Complex. The development of down-stream industries would be according to recommendations of the Centrai Task Force, and assistance from the North Eastern Council would be restricted to manpower development for the same and preparation of feasibility reports for specific recommended industries.

With progress of mapping and prospecting activities in many unknown areas in the North East there is always the possibility that new mineral deposits will be discovered and the blue print for future mineral industry development will, therefore, have to be reviewed progressively so as to extend the horizons commensurately with the developing resource potential.

8

DEVELOPMENT OF TRANSPORATION INFRASTRUCTURE

by
P. Krishnan

Inadequate infrastructural facilities for transportation has proved to be the biggest stumbling block in the development of the North Eastern Region. The coverage and capacity of the existing network of railway lines and good roads are insufficient to meet the needs of the region and the transportation links with the rest of the country are tenuous. The difficult hilly terrain coupled with flood prone rivers have stood in the way of rapid construction of roads and rail lines. However, substantial progress has been made in building up these essential infrastructure after the country attained independence. The North Eastern Councl (NEC), constituted by the Government of India to provide a coordinated approach to the economic problems of the region, has since its inception in 1972, laid great stress on the development of this vital sector.

RAILWAYS

Of the five states and two Union territories in the region, the existing rail network is practically confined to Assam with Nagaland and Tripura having just 9 Kms. and 12 Kms. of rail lines respectively. The States of Magahalaya and Manipur and the Union Territories of Mizoram and Arunachal Pradesh are outside the rail map of the country. Extension of the railway system is a basic necessity for industrial development. During the Fifth Plan, the North Eastern Council had financed the techno-economic surveys of a number of new railway lines. This has helped in expediting the sanction of the following new lines in the region.

Table-1

Sl. No.	Details of Lines	Gauge	Length (K.M.)
1.	Gauhati-Burnihat (Assam/Meghalaya)	BG	28.21
2.	Balipara-Bhalukpong (Assam/Arunachal Pradesh)	MG	33.45
3.	Lala Bazar/Lalaghat-Bhairabi (Assam-Mizoram)	MG	48.77
4.	Amguri-Tuli (Assam/Nagaland)	MG	17.07
5.	Silchar-Jiribam (Assam/Manipur)	MG	50.36
6.	Dharmanagar-Kumarghat (Tripura)	MG	33.5
		Total :	211.360

These lines are to be completed during the Sixth Plan and would provide at least one rail head to each of the unit in the region.

The existing network consists of 2110 Kms. of metre guage and 105 Kms. of broad gauge lines. The main centre for transhipment of passengers and goods from BG to MG is at New Bongaigaon and this has proved to be a major bottleneck in the flow of commodities to the region. Extension of the BG line upto Gauhati is in progress and is expected to be completed by the next year. This would go a long way in easing the transportation problem. At present there is only one bridge across the Brahamputra (a rail-cum-road bridge near Gauhati) and this would not be able to cater to the traffic anticipated by the end of the decade. The North Eastern Council has been vigorously advocating the proposal for a road-cum-rail bridge ct Jogighopa along with a BG line on the south bank of the Brahamputra from Jogighopa (Pancharatna-ghat) to Gauhati. It is learnt that the scheme has been approved by the Government of India recently. This project would not only give another rail crossing over Brahmaputra but also serve as a part of the second BG line into the region upto Gauhati which would ultimately come into being after conversion of Kalshar-Siliguri-Bongaigaon line from MG to BG. The development at lower Assam and the mineral rich Garo Hills District of Maghalaya, where a large thermal power station and a cement plant are being taken up, would be expedited by the Bongaigaon-Pancharatnaghat-Gauhati BG rail line.

The existing railway system beyond Gauhati, laid during the British days, with the purpose of connecting the tea gardens with Chittagong port, does not directly link the important towns on the south bank of the Brahmaputra such as Nowgong, Jorhat, Sibsagar, etc. In the interest of development of the Brahmaputra Valley and for convenience of the public, a direct line from Gauhati to Dibrugarh connecting these towns is essential. Such a line would cut short the rail distance from Guahati to Dibrugarh by about 130 Kms. and as it traverses through the plains, there would be further reduction of travel time. Survey for this railway line has been taken up by the North Eastern Council.

The limited capacity on the Lumding-Badarpur MG hill section is a severe constraint on the transportation of materials to the southern parts of the NE region. This 180 Kms. section having steep gradients upto 1 in 37 and a large number of tunnels carries at present only about 150 wagons per day. The magnitude of the problem can be imagined from the fact that the 300 tpd paper mill being set up by M/s. Hindustan

Paper Corporation Ltd., near Badarpur would alone require movement of about 200 wagons per day. Works for augmentation of line capacity on this route are in progress and with addition of more crossing stations, lengthening of loops and introduction of sophisticated electronic controls, it may be pos ible to increase the capacity to 300/400 wagons per day. Survey is being undertaken for a new BG line in this area and any large scale industrial development of Tripura, Mizorm, western Manipur and Caehar district would be possible only after the new line is constructed.

In course of time, it would be necessary to extend the rail network to the capitals of the various units in the region. NEC had carried out surveys for railway lines to Itanagar and Sairang (near Aizawal). A fresh survey for extension of rail line from Kumarghat to Agartala is also being undertaken.

ROADS

In view of the predominantly hilly terrain of the region, roads have to play a major role in transportation.

The National Highways are the main arteries of road communication. The NER had 2320 kms of National Highways and on 1st September 1980 another 1800 kms of roads have been declared as National Highways. However, a large length of the existing National Highways have not yet been brought to the required standards. A number of weak bridges on these roads imposes severe restrictions on the movement of traffic. It is necessary to have a time bound programme, to have all the roads declared as National Highways in the region, along with bridges on them, upgraded to the required specifications.

As already indicated earlier at present there is only one rail-cum-road bridge across the Brahmaputra river which flows for a length of about 720 Kms in the region and forms a major obstacle in the road and rail network. Realising the need to have more crossings on this mighty river, the NEC had commissioned M/s Rail India Technical & Economic Services Ltd. to construct a survey of possible sites for construction of bridges, and based on this study, a road bridge has been taken up at Bhomoraguri near Tezpur. Work on this Rs. 67 crores project is now in full swing and the bridges is targeted to be commissioned in 1985-86. Detailed survey for rail-cum-road bridge near Dibrugarh is also being taken up. Construction of bridges at Tezpur, Jogighopa and Dibrugarh along with the existing one near Gauhati would be sufficient to meet the needs of inter bank traffic across Brahmaputra for the next few decades.

While an ambitious road programme has been undertaken by the States/Uts in their Plans, the North Eastern Council has been filling up the gap regarding inter-state roads. About 1,500 kms of such roads were taken up in the Fifth Plan, and a-e nearing completion. In the Sixth Plan, the council proposes to take up about 1700 kms of roads of this category. The NE region is endowed with vast mineral and forest resources. Lack of roads has hindered their exploration and exploitation. Here also the NEC has stepped in and has taken up in Sixth Plan 1,600 kms. of roads to serve the economic needs of the region.

WATERWAYS

Inland waterways have traditionally played a vital role in the communication system between the NE region and the rest of the country. The natural waterways of the Brahmaputra and Barak river systems provided an efficient and economic route of communication between the region and Calcutta through East Bengal. Regular steamer services between Assam and Calcutta were plying since 1863 and were disrupted only after the Indo-Pakistan hostilities in 1965. The Central Inland Water Transport Corporation has now restored the sesvices, but they have not been able to attract the traffic diverted to other routes during the interregnum. There is, however, substantial scope to develop in land water transport within the region over the Brahmaputra ahd Barak rivers and their tributaries. The North Eastern Region has about 2,000 kms. of navigable waterways. With the rising prices and depleting reserves of oil, it is necessary to revitalise this energy efficient mode of transport. A detailed techno-economic and hydrographis survey is being undertaken over the Brahmaputra river by the Ministry of Shipping and Transport for improvement oi navigational facilities. A study conducted by the North Eastern Council has shown that there is scope for improvement of inland water transport over Desang, Burhi Dihing, Dhaleswari, etc.

AIRWAYS

The circuitous land link of the NE region with rest of the country and the difficult geographical terrain within the region imposing restrictions on surface communications, have given a fillip to air services. There are a number of airports in the region and air bus services have recently been extended to Gauhati. Vayudoot flghts have to play a major role in the NE Region. Even though a beginning has been made to have these feeder services with Fokker aircrafts, there are a number of towns haviug small air strips which can be served only by a short take off and landing (STOL) aircraft. A decision on the STOL aircraft to be purchased by Vayudoot is likely to be taken shortly and thereafter it would be possible to extend air services to a number of places in the North East.

Rapid development of the transportation infrastructure in the North Eastern Region is a *sine qua non* for the advancement of this backward area. Concerted efforts are being made by the Central and State Governments in this Sector. With integrated development of the various modes of transportation, the region with its abundant forest and mineral resources, and vast hydroelectric potential, is on the threshold of industrial properity.

9

SIXTH PLAN OF NORTH EASTERN COUNCIL

by

D.N. Chakravarthy

The Sixth Plan of the North Eastern Council as finally approved and now under implementation envisages an outlay of Rs. 340 crore which is Rs. 128 crore higher than the outlay fixed for the original Sixth Plan of 1978-83. With the announcement of new priorities by the new Government at the Center a major shift in the whole framework of the Sixth Plan became inevitable in order to reflect the declared objectives of the Union Government to fulfil the hopes and aspirations of the people of the country. The NEC's Sixth Plan also accordingly got reformulated in the light of the guidelines given by the Planning Commission. The reformulation of the Sixth Plan (1980-85) did not, however, basically alter the priorities the NEC has been following since its inception. This has been evident from the fact that transport and communication and power generation which constituted by far the largest area of NEC's sphere of operation since the beginning have together accounted for about 80 per cent of the total allocation of the NEC's Sixth Plan.

The North Eastern Council which has so far spent about Rs. 65 crores under Transport and Communication, is proposing to spend an amount of Rs. 155 crores under the Transport and Communication Sector for removing the inadequacy and short-coming in the field of communication in this region. The schemes under the Transport and Communication Sector include new schemes involving a total amount of Rs. 93.065

crores besides the continuing schemes of Rs. 61.94 crores. The new schemes to be taken up by the council include construction of roads of various economic and defence importance, construction and improvement of inter-state roads, construction of new bridges and surveys for the fourth bridge over Brahmaputra at Dibrugarh. The other new schemes relate to the setting up of Research and Development Extension Unit of the Central Road Research Institute and strengthening of inland water transport facilities within the region by putting navigational aids and floating Jatties in the river Brahmaputra. The continuing schemes under Transport and Communication include provision for construction and improvement of road and setting up of bridges besides completing the bridge across Brahmaputra at Bhomoraguri. The Council has already spent an amount of about Rs. 5.32 crores towards the construction of Bhomomaguri bridge and is making a provision of Rs. 40 crores to corplete the bridge within the Sixth Plan. Provision of Rs. 48 lakhs has also been made in the plan for conducting survey of the bridge across the Brahmaputra near Dibrugarh.

EMPHASIS ON POWER

With the pace of industrialisation gathering momentum in the North Eastern Region the North Eastern Council has rightly been imparting emphasis on development of adequate power on the basis of the vast potential available within the region. The Council is now getting an amount of Rs. 115 crores for Water and Power Development. This includes Rs. 71.65 crores in respect of the continuing scheme of Kopili Hydro Electric Project, Rs. 11.79 crores for continuing schemes of transmission of power from Kopili Project to different units of the region and Rs. 10.17 crores for continuing schemes like investigation of Kameng Hydro-Electric Project, Tipaimukh Project, Loktak Downstream and Tuvai Hydro-Electric Project in Manipur and investigation of 10 other Hydro Electric Projects. The Rs. 10 crore Garo Hills Thermal Project, Rs. 5 crore new Hydro-Electric Project (preliminary work) to be identified later, Rs. 4 crore transmission project in Garo Hills and new transmission project for supply of power to Arunachal

Pradesh form parts of the new schemes. The other new scheme include Rs. 2.50 crores for conducting investigation in respect of new schemes on major and medium Hydro-Electric Project and detailed investigation of 3 Hydro Projects besides investigation of Kyashi, Umtru Stage IX and Stage VI, one Hydro Electric Projection in Garo Hills and investigation of Makru and Irang in Upper Barak in Manipur.

MAN POWER DEVELOPMENT

A salient feature of the Sixth Plan of the North Eastern Council is the generous provision made for Manpower Development for which an outlay of Rs. 18.45 crores has been made. The provision under Manpower Development includes about twelve continuing schemes for various items like fellowships, short-term training schemes and setting up and strengthening of specialised institutions. The allocation for other important continuing schemes are Rs. 4.50 crore for Regional Medical College, Imphal, Rs. 6.30 crore for North East Police Academy and Rs. 50 lakhs for strengthening of facilities of Assam Agricultural University. The new schemes for which a provision of Rs. 4.02 crores has been made include Rs. 1.30 crore for technical education, Rs. 72 lakhs for B. Pharm Course in Assam Medical College, Dibrugarh Rs. 10 lakhs for Dental Wing in the Gauhati Medical College, Rs. 50 lakhs for Regional Ins:itute of Technology and Rs. 1 crore for other training programmes. There is provision for training of personnel in Tea and Coffee besides training in Industries and Mining Sector and for Lineman Training.

While preparing its scheme, the North Eastern Council has kept in view the predominently agriculture oriented economy of the region, remaining at the same time fully aware of the wasting practices like jhum cultivation that impeded the growth of agriculture in this region The North Eastern Council is proposing to implement a large number of schemes in order to bring about radical changes in the pattern of agriculture of the region. The allocation made under the Agriculture and Allied Programme which in total comes to Rs. 30 crores include Rs. 5.72 crores for general agriculture programme like setting up of seed farm for major crops, watershed management projects, (Rs. 4.50 crores) post reclamation assistance for jhum-control schemes, ground water survey and development and soil and land use survey. The new schemes under the general agriculture sector include Rs. 40 lakhs for regional soil conservation and staff training centre in Meghalaya, Rs. 10 lakhs for regional centre for training and production of mushrooms and Rs. 5 lakhs for establishment of a regional centre for production of bio-fertilizers.

HORTICULTURE SECTOR

The agro climatic conditions of the North Eastern Region which is quite favourable for growing a variety of fruits in large scale have prompted the North Eastern Council to take up several schemes under Horticulture Sector involving an outlay of Rs. 12.95 crores. The allocation under this sector includes continuing schemes like Regional Orchard-cum-nurseries and the setting up of a Regional Agricultural Marketing Corporation. All the continuing schemes will involve an outlay of Rs. 10.08 crores of which Rs. 8 crore will be for the Regional Agricultural Marketing Corporation. The new schemes under Horticulture Sector will involve an amount of Rs. 2 87 crores and will include provision like Vegetable Seed Farms in Assam and Tripura, Coconut Seed garden in Tripura, Survey of area and produces of Horticultrual crops in 7 units of the region, Development of Temperate nut and almond crops, Pilot plant for preparatiou of Pine Apple and Orange Juice concentrates, conservation and multiplication of orchids, pilot plant for extraction of starch from tapioca in Meghalaya and establishment of pilot plant for Dehydration of Ginger in Meghalaya and Assam.

PLANTATION CROPS TOO

The North-Eastern Region which has a world-wide reputation for over a century for its tea is now engaged in cultivation of different plantation crops like coffee, rubber and cashewnut. The region is also getting prepared to achieve larger production of tea by the close of this century. The Council has, therefore, earmarked a provision of Rs. 2.02 crores for setting up of clonal nursery-cum-Mother bush farm in Tripura, Factory for small farmer's Tea Estate in Tripura, Demonstration Plots in Nagaland, Manipur and Mizoram and Tea Nursery in Arunachal Pradesh.

The schemes under coffee plantation include Rs. 99.45 lakhs for setting up of 7 coffee nurseries and Rs. 81 lakhs for new scheme for survey and demonstration of land fit for coffee in 7 units, opening of shade tree seedig nurseries in 7 units and establishment of Coffee processing unit, Provision of Rs. 3.16 crores has been made for setting up of two bud wood nurseries in Assam and Tripura and 7 bud wood nurseries in all the units.

ANIMAL HUSBANDRY SECTOR

The NEC's schemes in the fields of development of dairy, poultry, piggery and other domestic animals and birds will include Rs. 1.51 crores for six continuing schemes and Rs. 2.29 crores for 11 new schemes. The significant new schemes under Animal Husbandry Sector include establishment of broiler chicks production and sub-station in Manipur and Nagaland mechanisation of biological production Station in Assam, sett ng up of Regional Exotic Beef Cattle Cross Breeding Farm in Manipur, Regional Buffalo Breeding Farm in Tripura and scheme for manufacture of Antigen and production of film for control of bovine contagious pluro pneumonia diseases.

The North Eastern Council which has undertaken several schemes for development of fishery in the region is proposing to spend an amount of Rs. 1.56 crores for two continuing schemes and 9 new schemes.

MINERAL EXPLORATION

In the field of mineral exploration also the North Eastern Council has been playing a vital role. It has been engaged in the task of providing facilities for expansion of programme for mineral exploration by extending new roads, to the inaccessible sites. The Council is now proposing to spend an amount of Rs. 3.20 crores for various schemes related to exploration of mineral and utilisation of mineral resources. The schemes under Mineral sector include Resources Survey by Remote Sensing and Airborne Geophysical Technique, Aeromagnetic Survey, Watershed Survey and detailed mineral exploratian and providing at a number of mine sites. In the field of large and medium scale industries NEC's Sixth Plan includes provision of Rs. 9 crores for setting up of Mini cement Wazeho in Nagalane, plant at Tezu in Arunachal Pradesh, Garampani in Assam and then another to be identified later.

SERICULTURE

Sericulture forms yet another important are a of operation of the North Eastern Council. North Eastern Council Scheme in respect of Sericulture confines mostly to provision of basic infrastructural facilities for the development of the traditional agriculture industries in this region, in general and Assam in particular. The Council which has spent an amount of Rs. 2.26 crore in different sericulture schemes during the last 8 years is proposing to spend an amount of Rs. 2.74 crores in the Sixth Plan for the establishment of nurseries for Muga and Oak Plant. Setting up of Grainage-cum-Training Centre and Mulberry Nursery-cum-Chowki Rearing Centre.

Another important area of NEC's activities for which provisions have been made in the Sixth Plan include Advanced Regional Medical Institute, Development of Pasteur Institute at Shillong, Strengthening of Forensic Science Laboratory at Gauhati and Brahmaputra Flood Mapping and Bank Migration Studies. The North Eastern Council has provided an amount of Rs. 5 crore for schemes under General Services and Rs. 1.55 crore for Social and Community Services.

The North Eastern Council provided an amount of Rs. 70 crores for its Annual Plan 1981-82 and is implementing an annual plan of Rs. 80 crores during 1982-83, it is looking forward for that day when developmental activities in this region will gather further momentum ensuring there by acceleration of the pace of economic development of this backward North-Eastern Region.

10

ROLE OF NORTH EAST COUNCIL IN THE UPLIFT OF THE REGION

by
Gian Chand

The North Eastern Region (NER) comprises five States of Assam, (87,523 sq. kms.), Nagaland (16,527 sq. kms.), Meghalaya (22,489 sq. kms.), Manipur (22,356 sq. kms.) and Tripura (19,477 sq. kms.) and the two Union Territories of Arunachal Pradesh (83,578 sq. kms.) and Mizoram (21,087 sq. kms.). The Region accounts for 8 per cent of the total land surface of India and has a population of over 26 million. The NER is a miniature India. However, on account of geographical isolation of the region and the policies pursued by the British during the pre-independence period, the recurrent natural calamites from which the region suffered, economic development of the area had been neglected with the result that at the dawn of independence, it constituted one of the backward areas in the country. It is only after independence that systematic attempts have been made to develop the region. More than 80 per cent of its population depends upon agriculture. The region continues to suffer grievously from the spread of pernicious practice of shifting cultivation. The land has very low productivity. Foodgrains and even common items of consumption like pulses, oil seeds, potatoes, onion, etc. are to be imported from other parts of the country. This is accompanied by the rapid increase in population, rusulting in large scale unemployment and poverty, as opportunities outside agriculture remained almost altogether undeveloped.

CONSULTANCY ORGANISATION

The North Eastern region was re-organised in 1971 and full-fledged states like Meghalaya. Tripura and Manipur were created along with Union Territories of Arunachal Pradesh and Mizoram. The North Eastern Council (NEC), which came into being in the wake of the re-organisatian was conceived as a catalytic agent to bring about integrated development of backward units. The Council which came into being on 1st August, 1972, following a Presidential Order, was formally inaugurated on November 7, 1972 by the Prime minister of India. Since its inception ten years ago, the NEC has emerged as one of the foremost consultancy organisations in the country and has built itself as an important technical guide to the constituent units of the NER in respect of integrated planning. The Council being an advisory body, in no way infringes upon the political autonomy of the constituent units.

Starting its programme of development with a few schemes involving an outlay of Rs. 28 lakhs during the closing years of the Fourth Plan, the NEC embarked upon a broad-based Fifth Plan with an approved outlay of Rs. 90 crores. The actual expenditure during the Fifth Plan, which was terminated one year earlier, was Rs. 54 crores. During the Rolling Plan period (1978-79 and 1979-80) the Council spent an amount of Rs. 65.33 crores and is currently implementing the Sixth Plan with an approved outlay of Rs. 340 crores. An amount of Rs. 114.48 crores has been utilised during the first two years of the Sixth Plan ending March 31, 1982.

Plan-wise outlays of the NEC and actual expenditure during the Fifth Plan and also the two years of the Rolling Plan are indicated below:

Year	Outlay (Rs. crores)	Actual expenditure (Rs. crores)
1974-75	10.00	4.87
1975-76	10.00	6.69
1976-77	16.50	15.86
1977-78	28.61	26.51
1978-79	82.85	65.33
1980-82	134.40	114.48

AGRICULTURE

The Council, at the beginning, laid special empahsis on the development of such sectors in which the region as a whole was suffering from severe constraints. The earliest schemes to be taken up by the Council related to strengthening the agricultural base of the region. Beginning with agriculture farms for production of certified seeds of high yielding varieties to be made available to the progressive farmers, the Council has sponsored the setting up of a number of fruit nurseries and progeny orchards to promote fruit cultivation in the region. Recently, as a result of the continued efforts made by it, the Government of India has set up the North Eastern Regional Agricultural Marketing Corporation Ltd. (NERMAC) with the objective of helping in the effective processing, marketing of agricultural and horticultural produce of the region. Similarly, the Council has also supported a number of schemes aimed at laying the foundation for rapid growth of rubber, coffee and tea plantations in the NER. It is also assisting in setting up a rubber and a tea factory and coffee processing factory in the region in a big way to successfully promote the growth of these plantation crops in the non-traditional areas of the region. The council has also, from its inception, taken note of the seriousness of the problems caused by the widely prevailing and harmful practice of jhumming all over the hill areas and sponsored a number of pilot projects to wean away the tribal farmers from this method of cultivation to settled agriculture.

As many as 5,295 jhumia families have been settled over 11,000 hectares of land at a cost of Rs. 5 crores during the Fifth Plan period. As continued efforts are necessary to reduce/control the harmful effects of jhumming, during the Sixth Plan period a major programme of wastershed management schemes at a cost of Rs. 4.50 crores has been provided by the Council for being implemented. Altogether 13 watershed management schemes will be taken up during the Sixth Plan period.

Another significant step taken was to investigate ground water resources and prepared schemes to harness the same. The NEC has spearheaded the setting up of a number of cattle and other livestock and poultry farms for improved breeding of respective animals and birds. Similarly the NEC has taken up a number of projects aimed at increasing the supply of fish seed and also projects calculated to control water hyacinth in fish growing. Recently, the Council has also taken up a number of schemes for development of forests.

However, the foremost single factor impeding the progress of this region as a whole ist he inadequacy of the transport and communication facilities. The NEC has played a significant role in convincing the railway authorities to extend the broadgauge line from Bongaigaon to Gauhati and also to set up six more new railway lines covering a total length of 214 kms. with a view to bringing Meghalaya, Manipur, Arunachal Pradesh and Mizoram into the railway map of India and additional railway lines to Nagaland and Tripura. The NEC also conducted feasibility studies for Feeder Inland Water Routes on the tributaries of the Brahmaputra and Barak. The Council has in course of the last 10 yenrs financed the construction of over 500 kms. of new roads, besides improving over 1300 kms. of existing roads. As the long bridge over the Brahmaputra at Saraighat near Gauhati has been found to be inadequate to meet the growing damand of the traffic requirements, the NEC explored the possibility of building up a few more bridges over the river. The second bridge over the Brahamptra at Bhomoguri is now under construction at a cost of Rs. 67 crores. It will be ready towards the end of 1985. It will remove major transport bottlenecks for the units like Arunachal Pradesh and Nagaland besides serving the heartland of Assam immensely.

The proposals for constructing a road-cum-railway bridge at Jogighopa with an estimated cost of Rs. 62 crores and extending the railway line along the south bank of the Brahmaputra from Pancharatnaghat to Gauhati have been approved recently by the Government of India. The NEC has conducted surveys for ropeways to link potential industrial projects. Altogether the NEC has sponsored and helped in the construction of inter-state roads measuring 1500 kms. during the Fifth Plan period at a cost of Rs. 56 crores and the approved programme for the Sixth Plan period involves construction of about 1700 kms. of road at a cost of Rs. 80 crores. Besides, construction of 1600 kms. of roads of economic importance has been approved during the Sixth Plan period at an outlay of Rs. 120 crores and has been entrusted to Border Road Organisation. The development of inland water transport, expansion of air services in the region have also been receiving serious attention of the NEC.

POWER

With a large number of rivers and streams the NE Region is endowed with a power potential of over 20,000 MW while the present installed capacity from all sources does not even touch 400 MW. The percapita consumption of power in this region is only 28 KWH against the national average of 135 KWH. Only 10 per cent of the villages have so far been electrified.

The Council has, during the past decade, sponsored a preliminary investigation of about a dozen hydel projects. The setting up of the NEEPCO and entrusting the task of constructing the Kopili Hydro-Electric Project which will have an installed capacity of 250 MW in the first and the second phases is likely to involve a total outlay of Rs. 120 crors when ready for commission by 1983. The project which was taken up for implementation by NEEPCO in 1976 is now in progress and the first unit of 25 MW. Besides the Doyang H. E. Project in Nagaland with a capacity of 105 MW and Kameng with a capacity of 450 MW would be taken during the Sixth Plan,

About 165 kms. long transmission lines have so far been completed and surveys and other preliminary works are in progress in respect of another 600 kms. of lines. During the Sixth Plan. it is proposed to increase the availability of power from the present 140 MW to 750 MW by the end of the Sixth and Seventh Plan, respectively.

MINERALS AND INDUSTRIES

In the field of mineral exploration, besides resource surveys by remote sensing techniques and aeromagnetic surveys carried out in areas of potential, a few other programmes like study and research for utilisation of available minerals for industrial purposes, techno-economic feasibility study for setting up for industries are also being included in the NEC's programme. The setting up of a few mini cement plants in the different units also form a part of the NEC Plan.

Development of sericulture forms yet another important part of the NEC programme. The schemes in this field include expansion of training facilities and setting up of nurseries for production of diseasefree quality seeds for muga, mulberry and oak tassar silk. The other activities in this sector include expansion of facilities for modern techniques of rearing and reeling.

To encourage traditionally famous colourful handloom and handicrafts, the North Eastern Handicrafts and Handlooms Development Corporation (NEHHDC) was set up. The Corporation has been engaged for the last few years in the task of developing fully the skill and potential for handicrafts and handlooms in the region, providing financial, technical and other assistance, promoting sales and improving the marketability of local products through the establishment of a network of sales emporia and provision of training and designing facilities.

EDUCATION

By now more than 2000 students have been offered scholarships from the Council for doing degree and post-graduate courses in various subjects while over 1000 trainees have been provided in-service training in various technical fields. Some of the existing technical institutes in the region have been helped to expand their facilities to take more students and some new technical institutes have been established. Recently, a project for setting up of an Institute of Science and Technology has been sanctioned.

Besides financing the setting up of Regional Medical College at Imphal with its present annual intake of 100 students, the Council has set up a Pharmacist Institute at Agartala and provided financial assistance for setting up of a Graduate Nursing College at Gauhati, a Law Institute for training of judicial officers at Gauhati and a Police Training Institute at Barapani near Shillong for training police officials of the region. The Council is also proposing to start a B. Pharma Course in the Assam Medical College, Dibrugarh and Dental Survey Course at the Gauhati Medical College.

Now that the NEC is 10 years old it can look back with pride on the initiatives it has been taking to bring the NE Region out of the clutches of backwardness and poverty. But the task is very tough and the goal is far off.

11

IMPACT OF IRRIGATION ON NE REGION

by

Dr. P.D. Saikia

The nature of the land holdings affects the economic efficiency of farming to a great extent. The most serious problem of Indian agriculture is the existence of uneconomic land holdings of the majority of the farmers. Small farmers defined as those with land holdings upto 5 acres (2 hectares roughly), constitute nearly 70 per cent of the total number of farmers in the country. The situation in North East India is much more acute. Though there is relatively low density of population in all the States and Union Territories of this region, the pressure of population on cultivable land is extremely high. The slow pace of development of both production and productivity in agricultural sector in this region can primarily be attributed to the inefficiency of small farmers. The tiny holdings cannot give them opportuntities for full utilisation of the available human and animal power.

Barring the hilly States of Nagaland and Arunachal Pradesh there is predominance of small farmers in other States of this ranging from 73.95 per cent in Meghalaya to 90.89 per cent in Tripura. It indicates the magnitude of the problem of the rural agricultural families in these States. Lower proportion of small farmers in Arunachal and Nagaland, however, does not reveal the real situation. In fact owneship of holdings in most of hill areas where shifting cultivation (Jhum) is practised is not very authentic as the land is owned by the village community as a whole. A family is entitled to practise shifting cultivation in as much as land his family labours can afford. Only the land under settled cultivation in individually owned.

A family holding is not a single consolidated farm. Each holding is not only small but also sub-divided into several fragments generally situated far apart. In the plains districts of Assam nearly 50 per cent of the fragmented holding is situated away from the village boundary. This causes farm operation difficult for the farmers.

The proportion of small farms in other states except Arunachal and Nagaland is extremely high. Out of the small farms of below 2 hectares of size, more than 50 per cent farms are below 1 hectare. This clearly points out the gravity of the problem of the small farmers in North East Region.

Agricultural Census data on operational holdings in Arunachal and Nagaland indicate the existence of higher proportion of medium and big farms. Perhaps the total area operated by a household during a Jhum cycle (3 to 10 years) is taken as the operational holding for the family.

Under shifting cultivation the farm size depends upon the working hands in the family. As the farm size is dependent upon the human labour the operational holdings are usally small. The average size of operational holding under shifting cultivation is one hectare only. As about 27 lakhs of tribal people eke out a living from shifting cultivation in this part of the country, they are all small farmers.

The proportion of small farmers is gradually increasing due to partition of families. Form the village survey and resurvey data of the Agro-Economic Research Centre for North East India, nearly 50 per cent increase of small and marginal farmers is observed within a period of 7 years. The NSS data indicate that in Assam the proportion of the operational holdings below 2.02 hectares increased from 74.01 per cent in 1960-61 to 82.63 per cent in 1971-72. The situation has further deteriorated in recent years. The Agricultural

Census data indicate that the operational holdings below 0.5 hectares increased by 24.77 per cent in 1975-76 over thet of 1970-71. Similarly the proportion of operational holdings of 0.5-2.00 hectares has increased by 22.43 per cent. Data on this aspect for other states of this region is not available.

There ars ample evidences to show that under the traditional system of cultivation, the small farmers can hardly improve their economic condition. A study on the problems of small farmers of Assam by Agro-Economic Research Centre for North East India reveals that the farms below 2.0 hectares could not provide a subsistence income for the maintenance of the family. Even the average family budgets of the households having 2-2.5 hectares of land are found to be only marginally surplus. These facts clearly point out that under the traditional system of agriculture, the small farmers cannot afford to have a balanced family budget. So the small farmers cannot invest in agriculture or allied persuits from their family income.

IMPACT OF IRRIGATION FACILITIES

A case study was undertaken in village Nahotia, situated at a distance of about 11 km. from the Jorhat town, the district headquarters of the District of Sibsagar, Assam, to assess the impact of adoption of improved agricultural technology by the small famers. Since 1973, the Nahotia Electric Lift Irrigation Project has been functioning and the farmers are utilising the irrigation facilities fully. Four electric lift pumpsets were installed to lift water from the waterlogged areas inside the embankment of the river Brahmaputra. This irrigation project was undertaken as a relief measure for the people who have settled in the new site as their original village was eroded away by the river Brahmaputra.

Before the installation of this lift irrigation project, the farmers were accustomed to the traditional method of cultivation. Only a few households used high yielding varieties of paddy without adopting other improved package of practices. As the village is situated near the mighty river Brahmaputra, they could hardly cultivate the winter paddy successfully due to frequent floods. Winter crop was also not possible due to lack of irrigation facilities. With the extension of irrigation facilities, short duration HYV paddy was introduced. The concerned agricultural officers demonstrate the package of improved agricultural practices among the farmers through demonstration plots and in this way, most of the farmers were convinced about the benefits of the improved practices.

One year after operation of the irrigation project the percentage of area under traditional Ahu paddy decreased from 54 per cent to 22 per cent, whereas the area under the HYV of paddy increased from two per cent to 32 per cent. With the availability of water and application of fertilisers, the average yield of traditional Ahu paddy per hectare has also increased from 895 kg. to 1,509 kg. and that of the HYV paddy from 1,843 kg. to 2,268 kg. In kharif crops also, the percentage of area under the traditional Sali paddy has declined from 80 per cent to 50 per cent, whereas the area under kharif Sali crop has increased to 130 per cent. The yield rate of kharif HYV increased from 997 kg. to 1,674 kg. per hectare. The average yield of HYV of paddy increased from 1,356 kg. to 2,199 kg. per hectare.

The land tenure system has, however, dampened the situation to some extent. The system of tenancy in the village is based mainly on crop sharing on 50-50 basis. Nearly 30 per cent of the operational holdings under paddy are leased in land. The share-croppers feel the insecurity of their tenure. The land owners now receive a higher share from their fields as the crops are grown under imroved methods.

After the implementation of the irrigation project and the adoption of improved methods, the annual average income from agriculture has increased from Rs. 2,737 to Rs. 4,018 per family, (an increase of 46 per cent) as is evident from the Table below.

Annual average income per household from Agriculture

Size Group	No. of Households	Average Income (in Rs.)	
		Before adoption	after adoption
Below 1 hectare	3	1,670	2,923
1.01.1—50 hectares	14	2,515	3,995
1.50—2.01 hectares	8	3,526	4,470
Total : . . .	25	2,737	4,018

The average annual income shown in Table I gives a picture of the performance of the small farmers before and after the installation of the irrigation project.

From the data of one ad-hoc study conducted by the Agro-Economic Research Centre on the impact of an irrigation project in Nowgong District, Assam, it is observed that most of the small farms have become economically sound units. Out of a sample 100 farms, 37 per cent were small farmers. In the year 1968-69, the crop intensity in the small farms inside the command area of the irrigation project was fouud to be 127 per cent whereas outside the command area, it was only 106 per cent. The yield rate within the command area has also improved substantially. The villages were revisited in 1974, and it was observed that both the small and big farms were engaged in the cultivation of HYV paddy in about 90 per cent of their irrigation fields and the yield rate was doubled.

In another case study the impact of irrigation and that of bank finance on the small farmers is found to be quite encouraging. The village Balijania is situated about 30 km. east of Jorhat town in Sibsagar District, Assam. The Agro-Economic Research Centre for NE India conducted a study on the village in 1977 and 1981. The State Bank of India has adopted this village for farm finance due to the newly created irrigation facilities from a small irrigation project. Out of the 60 households in the village 50 or 83.53 per cent belong to small farmers.

The average per hectare yield of autumn paddy of 29.41 quintals in the village was considered much higher than the local variety of winter paddy which was 19.16 quintals only. Almost 60 per cent of the households became self-sufficient in rise production. Another important factor is that most of the farmers including the illiterate ones could recognise and knew the utility of various chemical fertilisers and pesticides.

The small farmers in the hills are poorer than their counterparts in the plains. The administration of the State and Union Territories of this region are aware of he problems of the small farmers practising shifting cultivation. Some project are taken up in selected areas to introduce settled cultivation in dry or irrigated terrace fields. Terrace cultivation is proved to be successful in some parts of North East India, especially in Angami and Chakesang areas of Nagaland and some parts of Manipur. But in certain ecological setting terrace cultivation without proper irrigational facilities could not induce the small farmers practising shifting cultivation to accept settled cultivation. In fact many hill farmers abondoned their terraced fields where irrigation facilities are not made available.

The limited case studies amply proved that there is scope for transforming the small farms into potentially viable units through the application of new agricultural technology. The pessimistic attitude of the small farmers as is observed in other areas without infrastructural facilities is found to be totally absent in the areas under the changed situation. The irrigation project combined with the adoption of improved agricultural technology has brought about rays of hope to the minds of small farmers.

12
NEW STRATEGY FOR TRIBAL DEVELOPMENT

by
T.P. Khaund

FOR countries, the hill areas of north-eastern region of India virtually remained a *terra incognita*. So also were the people, unexposed to the rest of the world, and therefore, little known ourside. The general belief was that a god forbidden area inhabited by groups of people who lived a primitive life rough, fearful and uncouth. Barring a handful of people including a few social scientists and anthropologists, the vast majority of our countrymen did not, in the past have genuine desire or urge to know their brethern living in this isolated corner of the North-eastern region. It was only after the country's independence, the people in the rest of the country started showing some interest in this 'hidden land' and the people living therein. Some parts of this region, of course, came to the limelight due to external aggression as in the case of Arunachal Pradesh, and some others, because of insurgency as in the case of Nagaland and Mizoram. Be whatever that may, of late, there has been increasing evidence of the nation's interest in the life of the people, and their socio-economic advancement.

TRIBAL POPULATION OF NE REGION

The Scheduled Tribe population of the north-eastern region, according to the 1971 Census, was of the order of 43.43 lakhs, out of the region's total population of 195.81 lakhs. They spreadover a wide area of hilly and forest land covering roughly 1.81 lakh sq. kms., as against the total geographical area of the north-eastern region of 2.55 lakh sq. kms.

They are constitute more than 94 percent of the territory's of this region in varying degree. In Mizoram, they constitute more than 94 per cent of the territory's total population, in Arunachal Pradesh they are 80 per cent and in Nagaland more than 88 per cent Manipur's tribal population accounts for a little over 31 per cent and that of Tripura and Assam, about 29 per cen- and 11 percent respectively. Thus the tribal population constitutes an important segment of the population complex of the region.

HISTORICAL PERSPECTIVE

A very brief historical background of these tribes will be of interest. The tribals of the north-eastern region are its oldest inhabitants. There has been reference to those people in old literature and the epics where, as Dr. Suniti Kr. Chatterjee has suggested, they were called Kiratas. References to them were, however, not always complimentary, but they were spoken of fairly well in Mahabharata and some of the ancient tales. The most appropriate reference to the *kiratas* in perhaps the one in a tale of *Katha Sarit Sagara*. Mrigankadatta described the tribal king Mayavatu thus : "When the creater made you, be infused into your composition qualities borrowed from your composition qualities borrowed from your surroundings, the firmness of the Vindhya hills, the courage of the tiger an the warm attachment to friends of the forest lotuses". These people crossed into the region at different points of time and the waves of migration continued for a fairly long period. In course of time, the Aryans who migrated into the area much later and who happened to be a relatively superior group, dislodged these aboriginal people who, for survival, sought refuge in the high hills and the thick forests of the region.

The entire sub-Himalayan belt and other sides of the Patkoi range along the Naga Hills running through Manipur and Tripura upto the Chittagong hill tracts where it merges into the Arkan range is inhabited by tribal people belonging to a number of groups and sub-groups each having its own distinct culture, way of life and language. They all belong to a common group called Mongoloid. In the words of Dr. B.S. Guha—"Physically they were Mongoloid with light skin, of medium stature, developed muscles." They belong basically to two distinct language groups—Tibeto-Burman and Siamese-Chinese. A section of them, the Khasis for instance, speak the Mon-Khmer language, which is a branch of the Austirc family.

THE TRIBAL GROUPS

It will be impossible to give in this short article even a brief account of the numerous tribal groups who inhabit the N.E. region. We may only make a passing reference to some of the relatively bigger groups among them. Arunachal Pradesh has the largest number of tribes and sub-tribes totalling more than 100, of which the major tribes are the—Adis, Akas, Apatanis, Hill Miris, Khamptis, Mishmis, Monpas, Nishis, Noetes, Sherdukpens, Tagins, Tang sas, Wanchos, etc. In the two hill districts of Assam viz. Karbi Anglong and NC Hill, live the Karbis and the Dineach Kachuis. The major tribes in Manipur are the ones belonging to the Naga groups like Tankul, Lahupa etc. and the Kuki group. Nagaland also has a large number of tribes: the important ones being Angami, Ao, Sema, Lotha, Konyak, Sangtam, Chakhe-sang etc. Mizos, Lakher and Hmar are the major tribal groups who inhabit the Union Territory of Mizoram. Meghalaya has the following major tribal groups—Khasi, Jainth and Caro. In Tripura, besides the original Tripuri tribals, there are a large number of Mizo, Kukis and Mags, living in different pockets of the State.

A PROUD HERITAGE

The tribal folk has a rich cultural heritage of dance and music. Many of their dances are spectacularly colourful and rhythmic. And dances, to most of them are a part of their life. Most of the dances are performed on occasions of festivals which are related to agricultural operations—celebrated before, after or during harvest. They also have large repository of folk songs which are rich in their contents as well as tunes. Some of the tribes have attractive pantomimes. Many of them have lyrical poetry and narrative prose. The poetry, as well as the folk songs which are the spontaneous expressions of finer feelings and sentiment of these unschooled tribals contain fantastic imageries. One who reads the love songs of some of these groups, for instance the love songs of the Wanchos of Arunachal Pradesh, will be struck by their sophistication. Their fascinating tales centering round the creation of men, of bird and of animals, are examples of their developed prose literature.

Almost all the tribes have a proud tradition of art and handicrafts which are basically functional and are produced against a particular social or environmental settings. One notices nature's influence on their work of art and handicraft products, although some social influences are also traceable. Handicrafts are mostly functional made to meet mundane needs. But, the striking aesthetic beauty as well as the content and pattern of these works make them lovely pieces of art.

COMMON TRAITS

As indicated earlier, each of these numerous tribal groups has its own peculiar socio-cultural pattern. It lives, so to speak, in a world of its own. Each one differs from the other in ways more than one—socially, culturally, linguistically and also in economic status. Some are relatively more exposed to the so-called moder civilization. Some are relatively 'advanced' and others are 'backward'. These are differences in detail. But inspite of these, there are a number of basic things common to all of them and these basic affirmative are undoubtedly more important and impressive. All of them are surprisingly business like with a down-to-earth approach to problems and have strong commonsense. Simplicity, honesty and hospitability have been their treasured virtues. All the tribes are, generally speaking, endogamous. As one social scientist righty puts it : A belief in the importance of truth, a hardness of moral and physical fibre, love of adventure and exploration, a fresh, candid, simple attitude towards the problems of life are the qualities which the tribes can give to the rest of the world." Self-help, self-reliance and community spirit, which sustained them through the centuries in hostile surroundings, are evident among the tribes. If one tries to find big theology among these people he may be disappointed for they have little of it. But they have deep philosophy and a good deal of religion which has been handed down the generations.

CHILD OF NATURE

Most of the tribal groups live a hard life. It is an isolated life atop difficult hills or amidst dense forests with turbulent rivers and raving strems cascading down from great heights. They live with nature and are influenced by her. As Dr. Verier Elwin puts it : "For centuries the environment has been the real ruler of the tribals", the hills and forests around them provide them the landscape in which they grow. They have accepted this natural settings as the baby accepts its cradle. They love nature, obey her laws, learn from her and are always happy with her. Nature's beauty has gives them a line sense of colour and love, for rhythm. Pick up any handiwork of a tribal group you will find evidence of it. Their dances, tunes are also testimony to this fact of nature's tremendous influence on them.

SOCIAL STRUCTURE

There is a wide variation in the social organisation among the tribals of the region. But there are certain social feature, which are common to all. The society is generally patrilineal. There is, however, an exception in the case of the Khasis and the Garos of Meghalaya who are matrilineal, There is rarely any caste distinction in the tribal society although certain class distinction does exist. For instance, among some of the tribes one finds the chiefs as well as the commoners. The most remarkable thing in the life of the hill tribes of north-eastern region is the basically democratic structure of social as well as administrative organisation. Any dispute or problem between two individuals or between two groups are decided by popular bodies at various levels starting from Village Council upwards. In spite of the fact that there are institutions of village chief and clan chief among some of the tribes, such as the Nokma among the Garos, the Siem among the Khasis, the Raja among the Noktes and Wanchos etc. the democratic process at the grass-root level functions effectively and smoothly. With some exceptions, the land belongs to the community. These traditional social institutions are still strong and vigorous among most of the tribes because the system is suited to their genius and needs.

Social groupings are primarily based on blood, kinship and in some cases on locality. The village, for obvious reason, is the most important unit in the social set up. A Gond folk song very appropriately describes the importance of the village : "In all the world a village is the place for happiness". Because of closely knit family and community life, kinship plays a very important role in the social life of these people.

POLICY TOWARDS THE TRIBALS

There have been two distinct approaches or policies, advocated by two separate schools, including social scientists and administrators, in regard to development of the tribal areas. According to one school of thought, the tribal areas. According to one school of thought, the tribal people should be left alone-leave them where they are and keep them as museum specimens. The other school advocates their total assimilation and consequent detribalisation. Both these are extreme views and both suffer from serious shortcomings. Isolation in the precent century is impossible, nor is it desirable. Assimilation or detribalisation, on the other hand, will degenerate and degrade the tribal community robbing it of their vigour, vitality and colour. Between these two extremes of 'doing too little and doing too much', there is a middle path. It is, in a sense, a compromise between the theories of Boswell and Johnson or Russeau and Bishop Heber. This policy in India, was evolved by Jawaharlal Nehru who candidly put it in the following words : "I felt that we should avoid two extreme courses, one was to treat them as anthropological specimens for study and the other was to allow them to be engulfed by the masses of Indian humanity". This middle policy allows the tribals to develop according to their own genius. It avoids over-administration of the tribal areas and yet at the same time, wants the administration to provide the people with facilities for socio-economic progress. The policy aims at reconciling the traditional system with the aspirations of the modern age. It gives stability to growth and lends dynamism to Governmental efforts to improve the lot of the tribal people. It is indeed a difficult task and a challenging one. But then, it is the only sound policy for the tribal areas of the north-eastern region.

IMPERATIVES OF DEVELOPMENT

It is imperative to bring the tribal people of the north-eastern region to the level of the comparatively more advanced section of the country's population as far as possible. It is equally imperative that all the efforts, schemes and activities of the Government aimed at achieving this object must be based on the inevitable logic of evolution. While catapulting the tribal people upto the modern would, it must be ensured that they do not lose the balance but are placed firmly on their feet so that they can march ahead with a sense of pride and confidence. The procsss of balanced growth must not be unhinged. We must not interfere with the development-process. We have to guide it so as to minimise the conflicts that natually arise when a traditional society steps into modernity. In Pandit Nehru's words : "We must always remember that we do not mean to interefere with their way of life but want to help them live it."

POLICY PRIORITIES

Development policy for the tribal areas of the region has, of necessity, to give priority to material progress. Unless the material conditions of life of these people are improved, not only will they continue to remain cut off from the national main-stream, but will also remain weakling in the country's social fabric. Any programme for material development must be related and tuned to the people's cultural contest and social set-up. Undoubtedly food, potable water, health and sanitation, housing, communication and education are the basic minimum needs of these people. The important question, however, is whether these basic material needs should be met under purely welfare schemes of the Government as is the case now, or through popular endeavour as productive activities. Obviously the latter course is more desirable, and appropriate, for it will help retain the people's traditional spirit of self reliance. Dr. B.K. Roy Burman rightly emphasises such a policy of harnessing the forces of production and orienting the social relations of production in conformity with the tribal ethos of self management. The policy for economic development of these people has to take care of two important aspects—(a) removal of general backwardness of these people as a whole with the object of bringing them at par with others, and (b) meeting the specific needs and growth requirements of particular tribal groups within the larger tribal community, because amongst the tribal community in this region, there is a wide range of variation in economic standard and stage of growth. Therefore, a uniform programme may not lead to the advancement of all the tribal groups at the same time and to the same level. It has been estimated that roughly a little more than 90 per cent of the tribal population in the region is engaged in the primary sector of the economy and the percentage of those engaged in the secondary sector is negligible. This suggests that the people have a predominantly agricultural and subsistence level economy. Any policy towards the betterment of these people has to take note of this important factor.

BALANCED GROWTH

I would, at this stage, like to add a word of caution. In our enthusiasm to bring in faster material progress to the tribal society, the traditional culture of the people and the values of life must not be pushed to the background. It will indeed be a great tragedy if these people have to loose these great virtues and their rich culture in the wake of economic progress. If that happens they will hardly be better man—they will only be a poor copy of ourselves. Of course, they will be better off materially. Therefore the policy should aim at revival and strengthening of their traditional culture and all that is good in their ways of life side by side with material advancement. A balance has to be maintained between material and spiritual progress. It may be difficult but not impossible and should be done in the interest people themselves as well as in the large national interest. Let their culture and colour to the mosaic of Indian culture and vigour to our national life. As Pandit Nehru observed, the test of success of our policy for the tribal people should not be in the statistics of roads built, schools and hospitals established and industries set up, but in quality of man produced.

GOVERMENT POLICIES—THEN AND NOW

The British administrators thought it expedient generally to leave the tribals alone. There were a number of reasons behind the policy of leaving them alone. The task of administration in the hill areas was difficult and costly. Secondly, it was considered desirable to keep away the tribals from possible political influence from the world outside. Thirdly, some of the British officers genuinely felt that left to themselves the tribal people would remain a happier lot. The Scheduled District Act of 1874 had kept most of these areas administratively separate. The same situation was allowed to continue under the Government of India Acts of 1919 and 1935. The areas were administered as 'excluded' and 'partially excluded' areas. However, after independence the policy was abandoned and a new policy of development and integration was initiated. Basically, the content of the policy is more or less the same as enumerated in the foregoing paragraphs. The Constitution of India has made definite provisions for the welfare and uplift of the tribal people throughout the country.

Article 46 enjoins upon the State Governments and U.T. Administrations to promote with special care the education and economic interests of the Schedule Tribes and to protect them from social injustice and exploitation. Special administrative arrangements have been provided in Article 244 and the Sixth Schedule of the Constitution.

NATIONS CONCERN

A number of Commissions and Committees were appointed in the recent years to look into the problems of development in the tribal areas in the country. These Commissions/Committees recommended a number of measures which, if implemented in the proper perspective, will go a long way in removing the socio-economic imbalance and also breaking down the old psychological barrier which unfortunately still exists in some parts of the tribal belt in the north-eastern region. The Dhebar Commission (1961) recommended an integrated approach based on the minimum essential items like food, drinking water, employment, education, health and village roads. The Task Force on development of tribal areas constituted in 1972 suggested that the ecological occupational and social perimeters of the tribal population should be properly assessed for formulation of a policy and its implementation so that a steady flow of benefits coul- be assured to the tribal people. The Task Force put emphasis on improvement in the primary sector of the tribal economy. The Dube Committee, which submitted its report in 1972, tried to define a new strategy for tribal development should be defined at the national level and national efforts required for tackling it, worked out. It also suggested an integrated area development approach in consonance with the genius and aspirations of the people Recommendations of these and other bodies have in fact provided the basis for the policy of the Government towards the tribal people including those in the north-eastern region.

Also these indicate the anxiety and sincere concern of the nation for the welfare of the the tribal people and also broadly specify the administrative and developmental policy of the Government in the tribal areas. Protection of the tribal people is one of the primary objects of this policv. This, however, does not mean merely maintaining status-quo. In the words of Prof. Nirmal Kumar Bose : "The only safeguard required is to assure the tribal people of enough power to prevent them from being converted into helpless elements in a larger economic organisation which they cannot wholly comprehend. The only way to achieve it is through education and organisation, and the preparation to share with equality the burdens as well as the glories of a new Indian economy which we are all trying to make".

13

EXPANSION OF SOCIAL SERVICES

by

M. M. Varughese

The North Eastern Region is one of the less developed regions in the coutry. Regional inequalities characterize many developing conntries and the unequal social, political and economic opportunities constitute the 'problems' of the less developed regions. These problems, not being 'self-correcting' have to be solved through specific intervention. In doing so, one has to move faster so that the backward region is enabled to catch up with the rest of the country.

There is no unanimity about the type of development—balanced or unbalanced—which an economy or region should adopt. However, as our economy is concerned, the approach adopted in our Plan is very clear The development strategy followed in our country seeks to avert infrastructural bottlenecks as far as possible. This is the main thrust of planning in the North Eastern Region also. Many of the units in the region being late starters, the level of development achieved is lower than in other regions. While Directly Productive Activities (DPA) and Social Overhead Capital (SOC) can improve the economic performance of the regional economy, they contribute to the quality of life, indirectly only Modern economic thinking does not make a fetish of quantity at the expense of 'quality' Planning of social services assumes importance in the context of the emphasis being placed on the quality of life.

SOCIAL PLANNING

The question of social planning has aot received much attention in th country. While an impressive array of technical skills and achievements are there for everbody to see, our greatest failure perhaps lies in the arena of improving skills of the common man and of changing his working and living conditions. It is here that the expansion of social services assume importance in the North Eastern Region.

The expenditure on social services as a percentage of the total expenditure has come down from 21 per cent in the First Five Year Plan. This may be indicative of lower priority assigned to social services in the country as a whole. However the position in respect of the North Eastern Region is different. For the Fifth Five Year Plan period, social and community services accounted for 20.56 per cent of the total plan outlay of the State. This is exclusive of the NEC outlay on social services. The share of social and community services in the Sixth Plan outlay is 24 per cent. Thus the emphasis on social services has increased in the Sixth Five Year Plan. The plan outlays also have increased rapidly; and in absolute terms, the increase has been phenomenal. Against Rs. 189 crores in the 1974—79 Plan, the pro ision in the 1980—85 Plan is Rs. 573 crores; this represents an increase of more than 200 per cent. This does not take into account the substantial recurring expenditure which constitutes a large part of the total outlay on social services that becomes non-plan expenditure after the schemes get normalised.

PRIVATE EXPENDITURE

Here, one should not lose sight of the private expenditure on social services. The National Sample Survey (28th Round) has given out detaits about per capita monthly expenditure on education and health. The survey has revealed that private consumption expenditure on health for the country as a whole is roughly thrice that of public consumption expenditure, while private consumption expenditure on education is less than a third of the public consumption expenditure. Private consmption expenditure on education and health in the rural and urban areas of the N. E. Region according to the 28th Round of the NSS is as follows ;—

Table-I

Private Consumption Expenditure **(Rs.)**

	Rural		Urban	
	Education	Health	Education	Health
1	2	3	4	5
Assam	0.33	0.56	1.94	0.97
Manipur	0.65	0.26	2.43	0.45
Meghalaya	0.10	0.58	2.80	1.76
Nagaland	—	0.58	4.65	0.76
Tripura	0.30	1.00	0.20	2.65
All India	0.26	1.02	1.36	1.40

The above expenditure is exclusive of expenditure incurre on private tutors, doctors, nurses and midwives.

While the per capita expenditure on social services is generally high in economically advanced States, the North Eastern Region is seen to present an exception to this rule.

EDUCATION

According to 27th Round of the NSS, about 94 per cent of the rural population and 88 per cent of the rural population have no skills. The iteracy position is somewhat better. While this is the position at the All-India level, the position at the regional level would indicate the rapid strides made by the NE Region in he matter of education. While the percentage of of literacy has increased by about 8 per cent at All-India level, some units in the North Eastern Region have made more rapid strides. This is brought out in Table II.

Table-II
Progress of Literacy

(Percentage)

States/UTs	1971 Census	1981 Census	Percentage increase in 1981 over 1971
1	2	3	4
Arunacnal Prades	1.13	20.1	77.78
Manipur	32.9	42.0	27.66
Meghalaya	29.5	33.2	12.54
Mizoram	53.8	59.5	10.59
Nagaland	2.74	42.0	53.28
Tripura	31.0	41.6	34 91
All India	29.5	34.8	17.96

Except Meghalaya and Mizoram, the other units have registered ver impressive increases in literacy percentage. No doubt the expenditure on education constituted 47.6 per cent of the total expenditure on social services, while the social service expenditure in 1976-77 in the country was 22.5 per cent of the total consumption expenditure of administrative department.

Educational facilities have no doubt improved in the country. At the time of the Third All-India Educational Survey 24.4 per cent of the total habitations did not have a primary school within 1 km and 17 per cent within a walking distance of 1.5 km According to the position brought out by the Fourth All-India Educational Survey, 93 per cent of the total population had a primary school/section within ı km. If we go by the number if habitations, it is noticed that 80 per cent of them have a school/section within one km. Taken as a whole, only about 7 per cent of the popultion haue to walk more than 1 km to reach a primary school/section. Those who have to walk more than 1 5 km constitute only 5 per cent.

Lack of adequate facilities for education at primary level, particularly in some of the units, becomes clear from the above data. But it has also to be borne in mind that the terrain in some of these units is rugged and hilly and also very sparsely populated and the picture painted by the figures given in Table-III is not in any way depressing.

In some of the States like Nagaland, Meghalaya, Arunachal Pradesh and Mizoram, there is a preponderance of S.T. Population. There are Scheduled Castes also, though their number is not quite large. How these weaker sections in society are placed in the matter of availability of educational facilities is indicated in Table-III.

Table-III

Habitations of SC/ST served by school upto to 1 Km.

State/UT	All Habitations	Habitation predominantly populated by SC	Habitations predominantly populated by ST
1	2	3	4
Assam	94.09	97.18	94.10
Manipur	98.62	100.00	98.77
Meghalapa	95.65	100.00	95.88
Nagaland	99.68	—	99.69
Tripura	85.77	86.64	79.91
Arunachal Pradesh	76.44	—	76.84
Mizoram	61.96	—	61.96
All India	77.31	90.65	90.48

Inadequacy of facillties is noticeable in the case of areas inhabited by Scheduled Tribes particularly in Arunachal Pradesh and Mizoram.

The percentage of school-going children enrolled has increased over time ; the increase is particularly significant in the case of backward Staets/UTs which have a low base to start with. The substantial investment concentrated in certain units have led to this welcome development. The position in the North Eastern Region brings out the very clearly (Table-IV)

Table-IV

North Eastern Region-Percentage Increase in Enrolment (1973-78)

States/UT	Primary		Secondary		High	
	Class I-V		Class VI-VIII		IX Onwards	
	Boys	Girls	Boys	Girls	Boys	Girls
1	2	3	4	5	6	7
Assam	17.88	25.14	16.48	24.64	—20.61	—13.64
Manipur	—18.61	—7.95	—6.11	40.27	42.53	43.19
Meghalaya	14.10	16.46	20.29	33.14	23.85	50.92
Nagaland	11.68	18.50	23.85	39.61	58.02	96.01
Tripura	4.25	9.95	17.26	19.89	13.44	25.22
Arunachal Pradesh	51.79	97.25	133.82	268.43	436.27	307.94
Mizoram	0.76	1.69	8.57	13.74	25.97	42 83
All India	13.40	18.08	26.13	36.93	8.76	21 52

The efforts madc in reaching educational facilities to various units in the NE Region are quite impressive. Giıls' education has also been given added importance. Judged from the increase in enrolment, it can be concluded that no efforts have been spared for increasing enrolment in schools in this region. This region has no doubt received special treatment.

The efforts in reaching educational facilities to various units in the NE Region are quite impressive, Girls' education has also been given added importance. Judged from the increase in enrolment, it can be concluded that no efforts have been spared for increasing enrolment in schools in this region. This region has no doubt received special treatment.

The figures given above, impressive as they are, do not the whole picture. Some questions are still left unanswered.

What about drop-outs ? What about imparting? is the education that is being imparted stereo-typed ? Can we relate the education imparted with the local conditions and requirement ?

SUITABLE JOBS FOR THE EDUCATED

While the need for expanding facilities for education in the North Eastern Region is being increasingly stressed, how the educated would be fitted into suitable be gainfully employed ?

No doubt there are a large number of unmber of unemployed persons particularly in Assam, Tripura and Manipur, it would be necessary to create adequate job opportunities for them. If their training education does not make them fit for certain jobs, they can be imparted specialised training to make them employable. This would also highest the need for regulating admission for higher courses and matching the supply with the demand, in other words, manpower planning is a matter that deserves serious thought. Apart from the wastage of sources it solved indiscriminate expansion of educational facilities, without adequate arrangements for those educated to be fitted into suitable jobs or providing the wherewithal to enable them te be selfemployed, can be potentially harmful.

HEALTH

Expansion of education make people more health conscious. This can be partly due to the relativey inadequate health facilities already available in most parts of the country. The country has made considerable progerss in spreading health facilities. The crude death rate has come down from 47.2 (per 1000 population per annum) in 1911—1921 to 14.1 in 1978. The position in the N.E. Region is not in anyway alarming. though the region is backward judged from a number of socio-economic indicators.

Table-V

Death Rate-1978

	Rural	Urban	Total
Assam	13.6	7.9	13.1
Manipur	7.2	5.7	7.0
Meghalaya	11.3	5.0	10.2
Nagaland	6.0	—	—
Tripura	12.0	6.5	11.6
Arunachal Pradesh	17.3	—	—
Mizoram	—	—	—
All India	15 3	9.3	14.1

Except for Arunachal Pradesh, the position in respect of all other units is better than at the All-India level.

The per capita expenditure data on health and family welfare for the years 1975-76 to 1977—78 gleaned from the combined Finance and Revenue Accounts of Union and State Governments in India for the respective years revealing (Table-VI).

Table-VI

Per Capita Expenditure on Health & Family Welfare

State/UT.	1975-76 (Rs.)		1976-77 (Rs.)		1977-78 (Rs.)	
	Health	F.W.	Health	F.W.	Health	F W.
1	2	3	4	5	6	7
Assam (including Mizoram)	11.36	0.90	11.05	2.06	12 24	0.93
Manipur	24.44	.074	18.70	1.54	22.98	1.51
Meghalaya	35.45	1.14	31.62	2.13	39 98	1.85
Nagaland	100.47	0.03	98.13	0.19	119.98	0.26
Tripura	15.84	0.61	16.35	1.46	21.21	0.76
Arunachal Pradesh	41.90	0.02	57.31	0.22	5..15	0.17
All India	11.32	1.36	13.31	2.81	15.0	1.51

The expenditure incurred on health in most of the units is comparatively higher than at the All-India level. It is true that the figures do not really reflect the position as it obtains, as being thinly populated, reaching medical benefits to the far corners in the Region involves large expenditure.

HOSPITAL FACILITIES INADEQUATE

However it has to be noted that the rural areas as a whole are not adequately served by hospitals. These facilities are invariably concentrated in urban areas, leaving the rural sector high and dry. The problems become acute in rural areas where even private practitioners do not and cannot set up practice due to lack of patronage. In far-flung areas where villages are far apart and each village consists of a few households only, providing medical care is still more difficult. It is here that 'medics' and 'Barefoot doctors' can play their part. Assam and Arunachal Pradesh have taken some steps in this direction. All the same, it is a fact that the 'health' component of the social services outlay has been very small compared to the 'education' sector.

Yet another important factor militating against the spread of health facilities is the inertia on the part of doctors to move to the rural areas. The training of doctors is highly subsidised by the public exchequer and still any suggestion at movement to the rural areas is resisted. There is also absence of popular pressure for teaching medical facilities to the rural areas. Often State Governments/Union territories administrations are content with prestigious institutions at the State/UT capitals which can provide specialised medical care does not receive the attention due.

The control and eradication of communicable diseases is also one of the objectives of the public health programme. There have been deaths in the NE Region also owing to communicable diseases. Despite about 4 per cent of the population of the country living in the North Eastern Region and its low level of development, incidence of death due to communicable diseases is not very high.

HOUSING

Adequate housing, no doubt, enhances the quality of life. In the North Eastern Region, public sector involvement in housing has been minimal, Housing has not posed a major problem in this Region. However, in cities like Gauhati and Shillong, housing does constitute a problem. Setting uphousing boards with a view to tackling this problem can go a long way in solving it. It is also necessary to think in terms of designing low-cost houses, using local materials, suitable to this region, taking into account the general ethos and the tradition of the people. North Eastern Council has taken some steps in this direction At the moment there are no slums in the region; but it is difficult to predict what is in the womb of future. Therefore there is need to encourage private investment. Also provision of adequate house-building advance to the government employees in cities like Gauhati and Shillong may encourage house house-building activity.

There are many other areas of social services. But the most important are education and health. In these two sectors, generally speaking, the Region has not lagged behind the rest of the country. From the very small base, the progress made in recent times can be said to be spectacular. However, if basic social service is to be made available to one and all within a shoht span of time, the investment required would be colossal. This cannot be achieved without a conscious decision to revise drastically the priorities in the Plan.

14

PRESS IN NORTH EASTERN REGION : A REVIEW

by
P. K. Bandopadhyay

The North Eastern India presents a varying pattern of journalistic venture. The Brahmaputra Valley is the seat of Assamese journalism, while Tripura and Cachar district of Assam, predominantly Bengali speaking areas, are marked by mushroom growth of Bengali journals. Except Arunachal Pradesh other units of the North Eastern region do not lag behind. Khasi press in Shillong, Mizo Press in Mizoram, Manipuri Press in Imphal and Naga Press in Kohima are glaring instances. In Arunachal Pradesh the Directorate of Information and Public Relations, Government of Arunachal Pradesh brings out only one monthly 'Arunachal News Letter'. An attempt has been made here to deal with some salient aspects of Assamese, Khasi and Mizo exercises in journalism. The Press in Assam has got wide and deep roots, while journanalism in Khasi and Mizo dialects are nascent, though quite vibrant.

BYPRODUCT OF RELIGIONS PROPAGANDA

As in some other parts of India journalism in Assam started as a byproduct of evangelisation process following the establishment of the British administration. 'The Orunodoi' published in 1846 is the first journal of Assam and, for that matter the North Eastern India. It was an Assamese monthly edited by O.T. Cutter at the Sibsagar Mission's Press on behalf of the American Baptist Mission in Assam. The journal mainly dealt with religious matters. It continued till 1882 under eight successive editors.

Another monthly 'Assam Bilasini' came out in 1871 and continued circulation till 1883. Hemchandra Barua, the pioneer lexicographer, brought out 'Assam News' an Anglo-Assamese weekly in 1882. However, it was a short-lived paper and continued for only three years. 'Assam' edited by Kaliram Barua, also an Anglo-Assamese Paper came out in 1894. Some other papers like "The Times of Assam", 'Assam Bandhu', 'Lora Bandhu' and 'Tora' were some of the experiments during this period. There were also Assamese journals published from Calcutta, viz 'Jonaki' (1889) under the editorship of Chandra Kumar Agarwalla and 'Bijuli' (1896) jointly edited by Nilakanta Barua and Krishna Prasad Duara A good number of perodicals like 'Eastern Herald', 'Citizen', 'Assam Banti', 'Assam Bandhab', 'Benhi', 'Janani', 'Minar' etc. were brought out during 1900 and 1918. There were uncertain steps in the direction of sound journalism.

The period between 1918 and 1938 also show the emergence of a large number of newspapers, most of them short-lived. Perhaps the most important paper was an Assamese Weekly called 'Assamiya' published in 1918. Later, it was converted into a bi-weekly. In 1946 it was transformed into a daily under the editorship of Devkanta Barua. It was again reverted into a weekly in 949 and was in existence till 1958-59. Some important Papers during the per od include "Deka Asom", 'Awahan', 'Parijat', 'Assam Raji', 'Argha', 'Assam Review', 'Assam H toishi,' 'Shillong Mali' 'Tarun Asom'. 'The Standard' and the 'Assam Sahitya Sabha Patrika' (which is still in existence) and 'Bateri'.

From 1938, the Press in Assam got a sound foot-hold. A significant event was the publication of "Assam Tribune" as an English weekly from Dibrugarh in 1938. Later the place of publication was shifted to Gauhati and it was converted into a daily from 1946. 'Janambhoomi' was started as a weekly in 1947 from Jorhat and another daily 'Dainik Janambhoomi' came into being under the same proprietor. 'The Assam Express' another English daily came out from Gauhati in 1971. The 'Dainik Asom', a sister publication of 'Assam Tribune' is an Assamese daily being published from 1965. This year in February 'News Star', another English daily came out from Gauhati. After the Second World War. Shillong, the then capital of composite state of Assam saw some English newspapers 'Democratic Review' (published in 1953), 'Shillong Times' (1945) and 'Frontier Times'. Some important newspapers and periodicals during the period include "Agradoot" 'the only Assamese bi-weekly in circulation, first published in 1971), 'Asom Bani', 'Nilachal', 'Nagarik', 'Abhijan', 'Mahajati' 'Janamat' 'Ganatantra', 'Dibrugarh Batra'. Among 118 periodicals published in Assam 5 are dailies, 44 bi-weeklies/weeklies/fortnightlies and 14 monthlies.

IN MEGHALAYA

The spurt of journalism in Meghalaya is largely attributed to the strong urge of the tribals for self-expression. In Shillong the capital of Meghalaya, at present 25 journals come out. 19 of them are in Khasi language (two are bi-weeklies, one bi-monthly and 16 weeklies). The remaining 6 are in English (one is a bi-weekly another a fortnightly and the rest are weeklies). Twentyfour periodicals and newspapers came into being after the creation of Meghalaya.

Except one, these newspapers are run by the tribals themselves. The editors are part-time journalists. Political leaders, retired Government servants, college lecturers by and large, from the Shillong Press Corps. Except one weekly, namely 'Implanter' which is a cooperative venture all are proprietorial firms. The newspaper industry is quite underdeveloped and these are not run as business propositions.

These newspapers mostly have some district political tone. In this connection it is to be mentioned that two sitting MLAS and one sitting MDC (Member of the District Council) are editors of these papers. In some cases, news of socio-religious overtone are also disseminated through these newspapers. 'Kar Sur Shipara' under the editorship of a Rev. Father is run as an organ cf the Catholic Mission. Similarly "U Hynniew Trep" deals with the indigenous Khasi religion and seeks to preserve and promote it. Though the city does not publish any daily, these small language newspapers cater to the people not merely in the city, but also in the outlying areas. In most cases, the publication of the papers is so timed as to be sold at the market place where people from even far-flung villages come.

CYCLOSTYLED NEWSPAPERS IN MIZORAM

Mizoram shows another dimension of the Press situation. The literacy rate being quite high (69 50 per cent as per provisional figures of 1981 census next only to Kerala (69.17 per cent), Chandigarh (64.68 per cent) and Delhi (61.06 per cent) the print media has got a boost, specially after the creation of Mizoram as a Union Territory. As many as 17 dailies are published from Aizawl district (13) and (Tungki) district (4). There are also 13 periodicals (Weekly/monthly being published from the Union Territory. Of the dailies only one, viz Highlander' is an English and the remaining 16. that is 'Hun Thar', 'Harhna', 'Hmar Arsi', 'Mizo Aw', 'Mizo Arsi', 'Aw Thar', 'Zoram Tlanngau', 'Chhawr Pial', 'Ramai', 'Zualko', 'Ainawm', 'Tawrbham' (all from Aizawal district), 'Zeen', 'Jubitar', "Leitangputi', 'Zomawi' (All from Lunglei) are in Mizo language. These newspapers/periodicals mould public opinion and cater to the needs of the news hungry masses. All the newspapers contain only one sheet, that is two page paper, In the absence of a printing press 'Mizo Aw' is cyclostyled.

SALIENT FATURES

From a sample survey of the newspapers certain features stand out in bold relief. For example, in 'Dainik Asom' the proportion of the news items and non-news items is almost even in terms of the printed area. Slightly over 50 per cent of the printed area is covered by advertisements, announcements and miscellaneous non-news. The coverage and national and international items is also substantial. 29 per cent of the space deals with the national and international political items. National and International items are made lead news. The political items are the single largest news category (about 44 per cent). The social stories are not inconsiderable about 31 per cent). However, the coverage of economic stories is very poor (9 per cent). The local stories that is stories emanating from Assam predominate (68.3 per cent) of the political news. The regional item (That is stories emanating from other areas of the North Eastern Region) are hardly covered unless important or having some bearing on the regional and national scene. In the past few years or so the circulation of the paper has gone up and an estimated number of 80,000 people read the newspaper. The editorials, the stories, the manner of projection all indicate a kind of crusading spirit for the present agitation on the foreign nationals issue. The paper is virtually confined to the Assamese speaking people. It does not lose sight of the national perspective. The comments are applicable to the other dailies from Assam as well.

PROMINENCE TO LOCAL ISSUES

In Meghalaya and Mizoram the English Press primarily if not completely, deals with the local issues. Coverage of national and interuational issues and events is very thin. On the contrary the papers in the local languages give more coverage to the national and International items. The dailies in the local languages cater to the needs of the non-English knowing reading public who do not have access to the English national dailies. While the English papers are meant for the English knowing people who mostly subscribe to the English national dailies, The English papers of these areas appropriately avoid repitition of the items already read by the reading client. The language dailies have the obligation of supplying the non-local items to the non-English knowing readers. The local English dailies highlight the local issues and the points of view of the local leadership with an eye on the people outside the area, the non-tribals and the like.

The percentage of national and International items is quite high in both the Khasi weeklies and bi-weeklies and the Mizo dailies. The Mizo cyclostyled daily 'Mizo Aw' has devoted about 53 per cent of the printed area to the national and Inter-national items tnd 42.5 per cent to the local issues. The other Mizo daily 'Hun Thar', however, is more interested with the local issues, the percentege for the local item and national/international items being 75.4 per cent and 22.2 per cent respectively.

The Khasi weekly 'U Peitngor' has devoted 59.2 per cent of the total space to the national and International items while 3.15 per cent of the space deals with the local issues. 'Ke Pyrta U Riewlum'. a Khasi bi-weekly presents by and large the same picture. 52.8 per cent of the space deals with the national and International stories and 32.8 per cent of the space is devoted to local issues and events.

By contrast the 'Highlander' covers very few of the regional, national and International events, the percentage of space for the respective items being, 11.8 per cent for the regional, national items and 88.2 per cent for the local items

"DERIVED NEWS"

There is no network of reporters for the dailies, weeklies and bi-weeklies published from Meghalapa and Mizoram. The news, therefore, is 'derived news' collected from secondary sources except those items in and around the place of publication of the paper. From a study of news and non-news it appears that non-news items like advertisements, constitute a very sizeable portion.

LEAD NEWS

A study of the lead news reveals an interesting feature. All the lead news in the sampled copies of both the English newspapers, viz 'Highlander' and 'Meghdoot' deal with purely local issues. The picture is quite different in the newspapers in the local dialects. Of tho 83 sampled copies of 'Hum Thar' 13 issues carry some International and national items as lead news. The remaining 70 carry the lead news on absolutely local issues. Of the 30 sampled copies of 'Mizo Aw', only 13 lead stories relate to absolutely local issues. The remaining 17 issues carly International, national and regional items as lead news. "U Peitngor" shows a similar feature. Of the 42 sampled issues 21 carry lead stories on regional national and international events and the remaining 21 lead stories deal purely with local problems and events. 'Ka Pyrta U Riewlum', however, concentrates more on local issues. In the 13 sampled issues 3 regional items, have made lead news and only one international item has appeared as lead. The rest lead news are on local issues and events.

PROBLEMS

The newspapers in Meghalaya, Mizoram, Nagaland and Manipur are not run as real industrial enterprises. In most cases they are only a one-man show with small circulation. The owner is the editor, reporter and publisher. The publication of newspapers is mostly taken as a subsidiary income source and a means to wield power and cultivate relationship with the authority and also to express one's political and social views. Advertisements from Government, semi-government organisations, public sector undertakings etc. virtually provide the financial base for the these newspapers In most cases the owner has got his press and he undertakes other job work and the newspaper is only a byproduct

Lack of training in journalistic work is another major handicap. This is responsible for paper editing, reporting and general make-up. The need for training of the media personnel and the men of the Press, in particular, was strongly felt at a Conference of ths Central and State media heads of the North East Region held in February this year in Shillong.

Number of Newspapers : periodicitywise (Dec., 1977)

State/Union Territory	Dailies	Tri/Bi-weekly	Weeklies	Other	Total 1979	Total 1976
1	2	3	4	5	6	7
Arunachal Pradesh						
Assam	6	3	46	78	113	96
Manipur	12		3	29	44	4
Meghalaya	1	4	16	19	40	34
Mizoram	13	1	10	4	23	17
Nagaland			3	2	5	4
Tripura	13	1	38	9	6	43
All India	929	78	4,225	9,299	14,531	13,32

Source : India, 1979; Min. of Information & Broadcasting.

15

DEVELOPMENT OF TOURISM IN THE NORTH EAST

by
Rabindra Seth

The North-Eastern region of the country is as rich in history, culture and scenic beauty as any other part of the country. Today more and more tourists from all over the world are exploring Assam, Meghalaya, Sikkim and other parts of this region. In fact tourism in India gains a dimension and momentum in the eastern areas for here one meets the mountain and the sea besides the lure of the forest and the sight of mighty rivers. Here one can get to Darjeeling on the bed of the Himalayas for a startling view of the snowclad Kanchanjunga which always takes one's breath away, or go to Puri and read the oracle of the sea. Then one could take the jungle terrain to forests and wildlife sanctuaries, and the Sundarbans, the most wildly beautiful home of the famous Royal Bengal Tiger. From Watercrafts the sight would certainly bring ecastacy to tourists. All in all the vista is so varied and diverse that it can pack in the experience of a bigger India.

India Tourism Development Corporation (ITDC) has, over the years laid an infrastructure of tourism in this region, as part of the countrywide efforts which has considerably helped the mobility of tourist traffic and their accommodation. It has sought to help the tourist re-discover a great culture from the past as also a country making rapid and exciting changes to create a firm place in the world today.

ITDC is now making rapid in the north east region. The Pinewood Ashok in Shillong and Mayur Ashok in Gangtok

(Sikkim) are the latest ventures to provide much needed boost to tourism in this area. Many more new projects in Imphal, Agartala, Itanagar Dimapur (Nagaland), Aizwal and Kilasib (Mizoram) are in the offing. Most of these projects are joint ventures with the state governments.

THE LIGHT OF THE EAST

Lying in the extreme north-east corner, Assam is one of the rarely visited state of India, And yet, however distant it is one of most beautiful regions of India and certainly one of the paradise for the wildlife enthusiast, hunter, fisherman or naturalist.

Gauhati the Pragjyotishpur or the light of the East is the leading town and the recent capital of the state of Assam. It is known for its temples and shrines that include the Kamakshya and Bhubaneswsri temples which attract pilgrims from all over India. The famous silk producing village of Sualkashi is situated 24 kms away from Gauhati and has every household weaving the well known silk-Endi. Muga and Pat.

It is here in the state's capital that ITDC in a joint venture with the state government recently laid down the foundation stone of Hotel Brahmaputra Ashok. The 106-room hotel will be a three star property and will provide medium priced accommodation for tourists. The ITDC transport unit in Gauhati, the most convenient base for visiting the north east, provides cars and coaches. It also arranges tours to the famous wildlife sanctuary of Kaziranga, renowned for its one-horned rhinoceros.

From Gauhati to Kaziranga, it is an exhilarating journey of about four hours by road. Green plantations, tea gardens and rugged mountains are all along the road. Other species found in Kaziranga are will boars, jackals, buffalos, elephants and occasional tigers.

Right within the sanctuary stands ITDC's Kaziranga Forest Lodge which provides impeccable accommodation. The services offered in this 24-room lodge include a restaurant specialising in continental, Indian and local specialities and also a bar.

ABODE OF THE CLOUDS

Meghalaya means the "abode of the clouds" and Shillong the capital of Meghalaya provides a true glimpse. Situated close to the north eastern border of India. Shillong is one of the largest hill stations in the country. With its spectacular sun rises, its picturesque hills and skies and its multicolored tribals. Shillong is any visitor's dream come true. The 19-hole golf course draws golfers from all over the world. The Shillong peak a breath-takingly beautiful mountain offers a bird's eye view of the city. There is a unique zoo housing rare animals along with uncommon Assam monkeys, rabbits and deer. A number of waterfalls can also be seen in and around Shillong.

Sociologically Shillong has no equal in its variety of customs and religions as it boasts of being the proud of a mixture of many tribes. In this dreamland ITDC now operates Hotel Pinewood Ashok a three star facility with 55 rooms.

NEW DEVELOPMENT PROGRAMMES

Manipur, Tripura, Arunachal Pradesh, Nagaland Mizoram, are the other states which offer a lot to tourists More and more development programmes are in hand to, promote tourist traffic to these states and thus unfold the charm which till now remained a hidden treasure. Once again thus ITDC has emerged as a pioneer in bringing the north eastern region on the tourist map of India.

16

POPULATION TRENDS IN N-E REGION : A STUDY OF 1981 CENSUS

by
D.N. Chakravartty

The Five States of Assam, Meghalaya, Nagaland Manipur and Tripura and two Union Territories of Arunacha Pradesh and Mizoram constituting what is popularly known as North-Eastern Region of India has now a total population of 26,614 thousand as per the provisional population figures available from the Directors of Census Operations of the Constituent Units. While the actual counting was not possible in Assam, the population figures of that State has been estimated on the basis of what has been projected taking into account the trend of population growth in the State. With a total population of 1,99,02826 Assam has the largest population in the whole region, Tripura with 20,60,189 has come second while Manipur with 14,33,691 has come third. The population figures of the other States are Meghalaya 13,27,874, Nagaland 7,73,281. Arunachal Pradesh 628,050 and Mizoram 4,87,774. There has been a total increase of 7 mllion population from what it was in 1971. The decennial rate of growth during 1971-81 for the whole region was 35.92 per cent. With 49.73 per cent of population growth Nagaland showed the highest rate of increase of population during the decade 1971-81. While Mizoram showed the second highest rate with 46.76 per cent. The rate of growth in population in the other States and Union Territories were Assam 33.06 per cent, Manipur 33.64 per cent, Arunachal Pradesh

Population Trends in North Eastern Region

(Thousand Persons)

Census	Arunachal Pradesh	Assam	Manipur	Meghalaya	Mizoram	Nagaland	Tripura	All India
1	2	3	4	5	6	7	8	9
1901	...	4,290	284	341	82	102	173	2,38,337
1911	...	3,849	346	394	91	149	230	2,25,005
1921	...	4,637	384	422	98	159	304	2,51,239
1931	...	5,561	446	481	124	179	382	2,78,867
1941	...	6,694	512	556	135	190	513	3,18,539
1951	...	8,024	578	606	196	213	646	3,60,950
1961	337	10,837	780	769	266	369	1,142	4,39,073
1971	467	14,625	1,073	1,012	332	516	1,556	5,47,950
1981	544	19,903*	1,434	1,328	488	773	2,060	6,83,810

Sources : 1. Statistical Hand book. State Governmets/Union Territory Adminstration.

2. Pocket Book of Popalation statistics Census Centenary, 1972, Officc of the Registrar General, Government of India.

* Provisional figures.

Percentage Distribution of Population by Areas and Tribes, 1971

State/Union Territory	Total	Rural	Urban	Scheduled Castes	Scheduled Tribes
1	2	3	4	5	6
Arunachal Pradesh	100.00	96.30	3.70	0.07	79.02
Assam	100.00	91.18	8.82	6.24	10.99
Manipur	100.00	86.81	13.19	1.53	31.18
Meghalay	100.00	85.45	14.55	0.53	80.48
Mizoram	100.00	88.64	11.36	0.02	94.26
Nagaland	100.00	90.50	9.95	—	88.61
Tripura	100.00	89.57	10.43	12.39	28.95
Total	100.00	90.56	9.44	5.75	22.19
All India	100.00	80.90	19.91	14.60	6.94

Source : Census of India, 1971
Series I India, Paper I of 1972.
Final Population. Office of the Registrar General and Census Commissioner, Govt. of India.

34.34 per cent. Tripura 32.3 per cent and Meghalaya 31.25 per cent. Kohima district of Nagaland which had the highest population growth in the whole region recorded a rise of 92 4 per cent. Some of the notable population growth in the districts of the region are Dibang Valley 81.9 per cent, Phek 58.4 per cent, Wokha 52.3 per cent. West Khasi Hills 44.4 per cent, Nagaland North 52.3 per cent. Kangapal 43.6 per cent. Lohit 45.9 per cent and Siang East 43.4 per cent.

Population, 1971 : Rural and Urban

(Thousand Persons)

State/Union Territory		Persons	Males	Females	Scheduled Castes	Scheduled Tribes
*1	2	3	4	5	6	7
Arunachal	Total	467	251	216	neg.	369
Pradesh	Rural	450	239	211	neg.	366
	Urban	17	12	5	neg.	3
Assam	Total	14,625	7,714	6,911	913	1,606
	Rural	13,336	6,975	6,361	827	1,592
	Urban	1,289	739	550	86	14
Manipur	Total	1,073	542	531	16	334
	Rural	931	470	461	15	319
	Urban	142	72	70	1	15
Meghalaya	Total	1,012	521	491	4	814
	Rural	865	442	423	2	747
	Urban	147	79	68	2	67
Mizoram	Total	332	171	161	neg.	313
	Rural	294	151	143	neg.	278
	Urban	38	20	18	neg.	35

1	2	3	4	5	6	7
Nagaland	Total	516	276	240	...	456
	Rural	465	241	224	...	438
	Rural	51	35	16	...	19
Tripura	Total	556	801	755	193	450
	Rural	1,394	717	677	183	445
Total	Urban	162	84	78	10	5
	Total	19,581	10,276	9,035	1,126	4,343
	Rural	17,735	9,235	8,50[illegible]	11,027	4,185
	Urban	1,846	1,041	805	99	158
All India	Total	847,950	283,937	283,937	79,996	38,015
	Rural	438,856	225,219	213,636	70,441	36,721
	Urban	109,094	58,718	50,377	9,555	1,294

Density Decennial Growth and Sex Ratio of 1981 Population

State/Union Territory	Area (Sq. Kms)	Population (Persons)	Density (Persons)	Decennial growth 1971-81 (percentage)	Sex-ratio Females per 1000 males)
1	2	3	4	5	6
Arunachal Pradesh	83,578	6,28,050	7	63.51	870
Assam	78,523	19,902,826	254	36.09	900
Manipur	22,356	14,83,691	64	33.65	972
Meghalaya	22,489	13,77,874	59	31.25	956
Mizoram	21,087	4,87,774	23	24.75	936
Nagaland	16,527	7,73,281	47	49.73	867
Tripura	10,477	20,60,189	196	32.37	948
Total	255,037	2,58,90,404	102	38.76	921
All India	3,280,483	68,38,10,051	221*	24.75	935

Literacy Ranking in 1981 Census and Comparison with 1971 Census

State/Union Territory	Literacy Rate (1981)	Literacy Rate (1971)	Ranking in 1981	Ranking in 1971 (All India)	Percentage increase in literacy
1	2	3	4	5	6
Mizoram	59.50	53.79	4	4	10.90
Manipur	41.99	32.91	12	14	27.59
Nagaland	41.99	27.40	13	19	53.25
Tripura	41.58	30.98	15	17	34.22
Meghalaya	33.22	29.49	22	18	12.65
Arunachal Pradesh	20.09	11.29	29	29	77.95
Assam......Figures not available......					

The North-Eastern Region covers an area of 2.55 lakh sq. km. and has a density of population of 102 per sq. km. as against 77 per sq. km. in 1971. Assam has by far the highest density of population per sq. km. in the region (254) with Tripura coming in the second having 196 per sq. km. The density of other units are Manipur 64, Meghalaya 59, Nagaland 31, Mizoram 46.75 and Arunachal Pradesh 34.34 The pressure of population in this region should however, be viewed from the over-riding geographical fact of uninhabitability of the vast hill tracts, swamps and the perpetual flood-prone low-lying areas of the plains. There has been significant changes in the trend of density in all the units of the region during the last decade. In 1971 the density of population in the units was recorded as Arunachal Pradesh 6, Assam 186 Manipur 4?, Meghalaya 45, Mizoram 16, Nagaland 31 and Tripura 149.

The North-Eastern Region has now a woman population of 12,675 thousand against the male popu ation of 13,939 million. There are now 909 women per one thousand males in this region against the corresponding figures of 906 women per thousand males recorded in 1971. Manipur with 980 women per thousand males has the highest proportion of females in the region while Arunachal Pradesh has the lowest proportion with 961 women per thousand males. The State-wise distribution of the women population per thousand males in Assam 896, Meghalaya 942 Nagaland 871 and Tripura 943.

The North-Eastern Region has now a total of 9.8 million literate persons which include 6.4 million males and 3.42 million females. The literacy rate in the whole region is 36.7 per cent. With 59.90 per cent of its population being literate. Mizoram has the highest rate of literacy in the whole region while Arunachal Pradesh has the lowest literacy rate with 20.09 per cent. The literacy rates of the different units are as follows : Meghalaya : 33.32 per cent, Manipur : 41.99 per cent, Tripura : 41.58 per cent, Nagaland : 41.49 per cent, Assam : 36.00 per cent, (Provisional).

It has been seen that the rate of growth of literacy has been quite spectacular in Arunachal Pradesh during the last decade. It was only 11.29 per cent in 1971. The growth of literacy in Nagaland and Tripura also has been quite impressive.

A significant trend noticed in the 1981 Censuses as the rapid urbanisation in this region. The total urban population in 1971 was 18.46 lakh against the rural population of 177.35 lakhs. The last Census showed the urban population in this region (excluding Assam) at 11.20 lakhs. Among the towns having more than one lakh people, Gauhati is the largest with its population figure touching about a million. The Shillong municipal area has a population of 1.09 lakhs while the Greater Shillong city population is 1.75 lakhs. Imphal has 1,54,421 population whlie Agartala has a population of 1,31,513. The region has now altogether 127 towns of which 75 are in Assam. The population of other capital towns are : Kohima 40,000 and Itanagar 14,000.

Agriculture continues to be the main avocation of over 75 per cent population of the region.

17

INTEGRATED DEVELOPMENT OF NORTH EAST

by

B.K. Ahluwalia

The popular proverbial expression "poverty in the midst of plenty" does not seem to fit in so appropriately elsewhere in the country, as it does in the North Eastern Region of India. Embracing a land surface of 2½ lakh square Kilometres, the north eastern region accounts for 8% of the total area of the country and is endowed with an infinite variety of resources including petroleum on the one hand, and rare fauna on the other. More than half a dozen major rivers besides the might Brahamputra and its scores of tributaries, make the soil of this region with one of the largest reservoirs for hydel power.

But nature which has apparently been so bounteous to this region, at the same time, proved to be also the cause of many of its curses and overall backwardness. The geographical structure of the region, criss-crossed by numerous lines of hills, and endless streams of rivers made the communication to-and-within this region immensely diffcult. The geographical isolation also coupled with a series of socio-political and historical obstacles kept this region out of the caravan of national progress. No wonder when freedom dawned the people of this region were found to be educationally backward, economically handicapped, socially confused and politically frustrated. However, the rapid expansion in the filed of education which took place in the wake of freedom, exposed the people of this region to the glow of new ideas, which was pulsating the rest of the nation for decades earlier.

The political tensions which were witnessed in parts of this region for over a decade led the national leaders to devise certain effective measures as a permanent remedy for socio-political tensions and to accelerate the pace of progress of the hitherto neglected region. The national leaders in their wisdom, decided to reorganise the north eastern region, and to constitute a regional body styled as North Eastern Council look after the common economic interests of the different states and Union Territories, that have come into being as a sequal to the reorganisation.

The constitution of the North Eastern Council in 1972 may be described as one of the most significant events in the direction of planned and co-ordinated development of the five states and the two Union Territories of the North Eastern Region of India.

Although, at the beginning, there were certain misgivings about the functions and very utility of the NEC, the experiences of the last few years have proved beyond any measure of doubt the efficacy and wisdom of the setting up of such a regional organisation.

With a team of Senior Administrators and well known Experts drawn from all over the country, the NEC indentifies the common problems of the region, formulates specific projects and suggests implementation of schemes through the specified agencies.

Starting its programme of development with a few schemes involving a total expenditure of Rs. 28.00 lakhs during the closing years of the Fourth Plan, the NEC embarked upon a broad based Fifth Plan with an approved outlay of Rs. 90.00 crores. The actual expenditure during Plan period were Rs. 4.86 crores, Rs. 6.89 crores, Rs. 15.85 crores and Rs. 26.5 crores respectively during the four Annual Plans from 1974-75 to 1977-78. With a total expenditure of Rs. 22 crores, water and power development received the highest priority during the four years of the Fifth Plan, while transport and communication received the second highest priority with a total expenditure of about Rs. 11 crores. Agriculture and allied sectors involved an outlay of Rs. 9.36 crores during the Fifth Plan which was terminated one year earlier. The actual expenditure during the 4 years of the Fifth Plan accounted for 83% of the total allocation of over Rs. 65.00 crores.

The outlay of Rs. 212 crores approved for the original Sixth Plan of NEC included Rs. 100.49 crores for water and power development, Rs. 75.00 crores for transport and communication, Rs. 24.00 crores for agriculture and allied programmes, Rs. 6.02 crores for industry and mining and Rs. 2.20 crores for general services.

The NEC has rightly been imparting top priority to the programme of power generation since the process of modernisation could never be ushered in without the development of adequate power. With the present power generation from all sources in the region not reaching even 400 MW and with the prospects of a big power shortage of over 500 MW by 1990, the NEC is engaged in the task of exploring the possibility of harnessing effectively the water resources and generating power from different other sources. The Kopili Project with the total capacity of generating 250 MW of power and having the possible involvement of Rs. 120 crores in the first stage is by the biggest scheme sponsored by the NEC. Besides working for the thermal based Power Station in Garo Hills which is likely to generate 120 MW of power at a cost of Rs. 77 crores, the NEC has also been extending financial assistance for investigation of several prospective power projects, including those of Ranganadi, Papu, Damwe and Tuivai which will involve an over-all cost of Rs. 600 crores when ready for commission.

Removal of the inadequacy and shortcomings of communication is one of the major tasks the NEC has been engaged with. It is now known to all how it has been playing a vital role in getting through the project of extending the broad-gauge line from Bongaigaon and also in convincing the Government of India of the urgency of setting up six more new railway lines for linking the units like Nagaland, Meghalaya, Arunachal Pradesh, Mizoram and Tripura with Railway. With a view to exploring the possibility of starting a feeder inland water route on the tributaries of Brahamputra and Barak the NEC has also been conducting a feasibility study. The NEC has already implemented in all the states and Union Territories scores of schemes for construction of new roads of regional importance and in the meanwhile built up 500 Km. of roads throughout the region. A second bridge over the river Brahamputra at Bhomoraguri sponsored by the NEC will impart a new dimension to the communication system of this region when it will be completed by 1985 at a cost of about Rs. 40 crores. A third bridge of the river Brahamputra at Jogighopa and another in Upper Assam are likely to come up by the close of the century thanks to the persistant efforts of the NEC and the Governments of the States and Union Territories in this region. Third level air lines are also coming soon.

Agriculture in North Eastern Region being largely practised in the traditional way and aggravated by wide prevalence of wasting system called jhum cultivation, needs immediate reorganisation. The NEC has played a significant role in weaning away the tribal peasants from the old practices of jhuming and also in introducing the modern methods in the agricultural system through the introduction of packages of improved practices, popularisation of use of improved seeds and regular supply of inputs.

The schemes under the NEC in the agricultural sector include among others rectification of problems of shifting cultivation arrangement of short-term courses in agriculture and allied subjects, expansion of training facilities in Assam Agricultural University and allied subjects, expansion of training facilities in Assam Agricultural University and setting up of a number of Foundation Seed Farms for various corps.

LARGE SCALE FRUITS PRODCUTION

The ideal agro-climatic conditions of the North Eastern Region for growing a variety of fruits in large scale have been studied by the NEC and it has in the meanwhile set up a number of fruit nurseries in the hills and plains of this region. Several new schemes under the Horticultural Section when fully implemented would provide a stable base of uplifting the economic condition of a large section of the society in the North Eastern India.

While this region has world-wide reputation for over a century for its tea and recently for jute it is also taking up the cultivation of different plantation crops like coffee, rubber and cashewnut. The NEC is, therefore, stepping in the new fields gradually and going to establish nurseries in the constitutent units for growing coffee, rubber and such other plantation crops.

The Planning Commission has recommended a new scheme for tea nurseries and demonstration plots in this region, accepting high potential of tea production in this region. Steps are also in progress for setting up of the regional Agricultural Marketing Corporation for promotion for markets and related matters pertaining to agricultural, horticultural and animal products of this region

The Council also has taken initiative in the field of detailed survey in selected areas of this region with a view to embarking upon a large scale programme of reclamation and development of land for the purpose of agriculture. The scheme for ground water survey and exploration in parts of Assam, Meghalaya, Tripura and Manipur had been taken up during the 5th Plan Period.

NEC's schemes in the field of development of dairy, poultry, piggery and other domestic animals and birds include the setting up of Regional Breeding Farms for cattle, pigs, sheep and other animals. The Biological Products Station at Khanapara Veterinary Complex is another projeet financed by the NEC.

Although Assam, Tripura and Manipur provide ideal conditions for fishery there is inadequacy of fish to meet the growing demand. The NEC has undertaken schemes for setting up of Regional Fish Seed Farm in Nagaland, High Altitude Fish Seed Farm in Arunachal Pradesh, Regional Fish Pituitary gland Bank in Tripura, Survey of Beels and development of fishery in Nowgong district of Assam.

A few more schemes like aqua culture potentialities on Takmu Fisheries in Manipur, 'demonstration project on aquatic weed control' near Gauhati and a 'regional grass carp and exotic fish seed farm' have also been taken up.

In the field of mineral exploration also, the North Eastern Council is playing a pivotal role. It has been engaged in the task of providing facilities for expansion of the programme of mineral exploration by extending new roads to the inaccessible sites. An aeromagnetic survey has also been undertaken through National Remote Sensing Agency and NGRI. Along with exploration, is proceeding the programme of study and research for utilisation of available minerals for industrial purpose. Setting up of mini cement plants in suitable areas of the region also forms a part of NEC Plan. The first mini cement plant is coming up within 1982 at Tezu in Arunachal Pradesh at a total cost of Rs. 86 lakhs.

Sericulture consitutes yet another important sector of the North Eastern Council Plan. The programme in this field includes expansion of training facilities and setting up of Muga, Oak Sassar and mulberry nurseries for promotion of more systematic and improved method of rearing and spinning.

With the beauty and glory of its handicrafts and handlooms wares, the North Eastern Region has great scope for developing such traditional crafts which are, however, facing challenges from sophisticated markets and need patronage. The North Eastern Council has played a significant role in the setting up of the North East Handicrafts and Handlooms Corporation to take up the task of promoting market for handicraft and handloom products and for improving their designs and textures.

A few Regional Institutes also owe their origin to the North Eastern Council. The Regional Medical College at Imphal with a present annual intake of 75 students, Regional Graduate Nursing College, Gauhati with its intake of 50 students and Regional College of Physical Education with an in-take of 40 students form part of the NEC sponsored institutions.

The North Eastern Police Academy at Barapani in Meghalaya is also a NEC sponsored scheme for training police personnel of this region. The Forensic Laboratory of Gauhati is being strengthened with assistance from North Eestern Council.

Besides organising courses in specialised fields like diamond drilling, cement production, vaccine production and Handloom-Handicrafts production the NEC has sponsored higher education for about 1200 students In 162 short term professional courses, provided scholarships to a large number of students for prosecuting studies in agriculture and veterinary science. It is also financing students in prosecuting studies in Management and a few specialised technical courses.

Under the new 6th Plan as proposed by the NEC Secretariat an over-all expenditure of Rs. 445.86 crores is envisaged in order to accelerate the develepment of power, transport facilities, expansion of production of Agriculture, Animal Husbandry, Fishery and Sericulture and development of manpower. The Council proposes to spend an amount of Rs. 185 crores in the Road sector which includes completion of the Brahmaputra Bridge at Bhomoraguri and detailed survey for a bridge over Brahmaputra at Bogibil near Dibrugarh. The different schemes proposed during the 6th Plan include surveys for new Railway lines, inland water transport, construction of roads and setting up of a Research and Development Extension unit of the Central Road Research Institute. The programme under Power development related mainly to the completion of the Kopil Hydel Project, commencement of construction of a new hydel project and conducting of a number of surveys and investigations.

The new schemes proposed; under a few other sectors like Agriculture, Mineral Development, Horticulture, Animal Husbandry and Sericulture are expected to pave the way for building up of a dependable infrastructure to support a new momnetum in the economic activities in the entire North East Region.

NAGALAND

The people of Naga Hills which were part of the then Assam State had been demanding an independent Nagaland. The Centre made it clear that it was not going to let it happen. Some Naga leaders saw reason in Nagaland continuing as an integral part of India and others took to violence. Political situation of the Naga Hills had been full of only fear, suspicion and the spirit of revenge. Then Naga Peoples' Council was set up in 1957 and the 16 point Agreement signed between the Naga People and the Government of India in 1959. One of the points was creation of the Sixteenth State of the Indian Union to be called Nagaland. On December 1, 1963 the new State was inaugurated at Kohima by then President Dr. S. Radhakrishnan. Nineteen years after cessation of open armed conflict and six years after Shillong Accord of 1975 peace prevails in the State.

Nagaland completed 22 years of Statehood on first December 1982. This beautiful and eastern most State of India, little known to the outsider till recently has made good strides in various fields.

AGRICULTURE

Nagaland is an agricultural State. Except in Kohima and Phek district, *Jhum* cultivation is extensively practised. To wean away the farmers from *jhumming* the benefits of permanent cultivation are being demonstrated through schemes like pilot projects, watershed management and small scale demonstration, etc. Experts from Angami and Chakesang areas visit other parts of Nagaland to demonstrate the technique of terraced rice cultivation to the farmers.

Farmers are also encouraged to raise fruit and cash crops. Coffee cultivation is gaining popularity among the farmers due to the joint efforts of the State Plantation Corporation and the Coffee Board. Sugarcane is the important cash crop at Dimapur where sugar mills are established. High yielding varieties of seeds, fertilizers, pesticides, etc. are being supplied to help boost productivity.

Under minor irrigation programme, surface water is being exploited and efforts to tap ground water in progress. Central Ground Water Board has taken up systematic survey and exploratory works in the foothill area of the State. Lift Irrigation projects for utilising the water of the rivers like Kidhu, Milak, Dhansiri are being taken up. An Investigation Cell is drawing a master plan for irrigation.

To build up technical manpower every year a good number of local candidates are sent for higher studies. One agricultural college at Medziphema has already been established under the North Eastern Hill University. A number of in-service officers are deputed for further studies according to need and demand.

ANIMAL HUSBANDRY AND VETERNINARY SERVICES

Under the animal husbandry development programmes greater emphasis has been laid on poultry, cattle, piggery, sheep and goat development. The four cattle breeding farms at Lierie, Medziphema, Aliba and Tuensang were strengthened and expanded and the strength of milch cows was raised to 300. For intensification of cattle development 38 Stockman Centres were set up at the village level.

The existing five pig breeding centres at Medziphema, Merangkongg, Akuloto, Tuensang ann Tijit were strengthened by increasing the breeding stock to a total of 500 sows. Under the Centrally Sponsored Cross-breed Piggery Production Scheme, 2400 piggery units, each consisting of three animals were established in 65 villages covering 2400 farmers.

There are already 27 veterniary dispensaries, 43 veterniary out posts, 9 quarantine check posts, 10 mobile veterniary dispensaries, one disease investigation and control centre at the village level for rendering better treatment facilities to the livestock in the rural areas. Mass vaccination against swine fever, foot and mouth disease, rinderpest are carried out from time to time. One V.F.A. Training Institute has been set up and sixteen students on V.F.A. source came out successful. A new batch of eight students were admtted.

EDUCATION

There are eight degree colleges of which seven colleges are fully government managed and the rest are recognised and aided ones. All these colleges are affiliated to the North Eastern Hill University with its headquarters at Shillong in Meghalaya. Two new colleges one at Kohima and the other at Pfutsero are being opened.

One university campus functions at Kohima where post-graduate courses in English education and commerce are offered. A Law College has been functioning at Kohima since 1978-79 and has shown good results.

The Nagaland College of Education is the only college for imparting training to teachers for both M.Ed. and Under-Graduate courses. State Council of Educational Research and Training has been set up in the Nagaland College of Education with effect from 1st December, 1979.

There are altogether 97 high schools, 285 middle schools and 1109 primary schools. The number of government schools and High schools 50, M.E. Schools 202 and L.P. school 1063. Overall student-teacher ratio is 25.1. As on March 31, 1981 there were 1,50,00 Students at the primary school level.

Except Agricultural College at Medziphema established in 1978 there is no engineering or technical college in the State. The only technical Education institute is the Nagaland Polytechnic, situated at Atoizu in Zunheboto District. It offers diplomas in civil, mechnical and eleetrical enginnering with an intake capacity of 60 trainees.

The only Industrial Training Institute at Kohima has provision for imparting training in over a dozen trades of which tailoring is entirely for women.

The three Junior Teachers' Training Institutes at Chiechama, Yimyu (Mokokchung) and Tuensang provide in-service (one year certificate course) to primary teachers, conduct orientation courses and are centres of continuation education as well, The intake capacity of each of these institutions has been raised from 100 to 120 last year.

ELECTRICITY

Over the past two years a record number of villages and towns have been electrified bringing the up-to-date total number of villages electrified in Nagaland to 437. This shows that 45 per cent of total number of villages have been electrified sofar and this compares favovrably with other developed states in the country.

Dzudza Hydro Electric Project, the first hydel power project in Nagaland was commissioned on 29th March 1978. The project has an installed capacity of 1.5 MW. This seasonal power station is running satisfactorily supplying power to Kohima and its adjoining areas during monsoon period. At Kohima Sub-Station, a separate arrangement has been made to supply electricity to Wokower and Phek districts through the existing transmission line from this station.

Water power studies and preparation of detailed report for the 105 Doyang Hydel Project has been completed and the Contre's green signal is awaited.

Dikhu Micro Hydel Project near Mokokchung with an installed capacity of 1 KW at an estimated cost of Rs. 155—lakh has been cleared by Central Electricity authority. It is likely to be completed by 1983.

Rural Electrification Programme has been stepped up with increased plan outlay. The outlay for 1981-82 was Rs. 100 lakh out of which Rs. 52 lakh were under State Plan and the rest under R.E.C. and M.N.P. pragramme.

A feasibility report for a 30 KW thermal power station at the pit head of the Borjan Colliery, has been prepared and submitted to the Central Electricity Authority for clearance.

The present unrestricted demand of power in the State is about 10 MW. Assam is able to give hardly 6 MW on account of the current disturbances in Assam. A total of about 1.5 MW only is generated during peak hours from the standby diesel generating stations in the major towns of the State.

Dzudza Micro Hydel Project adds another 1 MW during rainy season.

With the commissioning of one diesel station at Dimapur, the peak availability has been further increased by 1.5 MW. Inspite of all this additional generation, power demand in the State is increasing so rapidly that the peak demand can hardly be met. Load restrictions, therefore, may have to be continued for some industrial consumers.

With the commissioning of the 132 KV line and associated substations early this year the position of power availability has improved considerably.

GEOLOGY AND MINING

The Department of Geology & Mining have discovered some important mineral deposits which in due course may provide a base for establishing mineral based industries.

The discovery includes vast reserves of high grade limestone, sizeable resources of coal, multi-metal-deposit of chromium-nickel-cobalt cearing magnetite and encouraging prospect of polymetallic sulphate mineralisation. Besides these deposits of clay, slate, and glass sand have been recorded at a number of places in the State.

In order to properly manage the vast mineral resources which are now being identified in Nagaland, the Nagaland State Mineral Development Corporation has been registered in 1981 and preliminary stepts are now being taken for exploitation of the various minerals in the state.

PETROLEUM

Oil and Natural Gas Commission have so far completed exploratory Drilling of three wells in Champang/Tsore area of Wokha district. A trial production of approximately 75 tonnes (90 to 93 kilolitres) per day of crude oil has commenced and is continuing in one of these wells since March 1981. Besides developing the above oilfield, the O.N.G.C has also drawn up an ambitious programme of exploration all along the foothill areas of the State.

FOREST

Out of the total land area of 16,52,700 hectares forests occupy approximately 2,86,137 ha. of which reserved forest extent over 27,141 ha. ; protected forest 51,790 ha. and private forest 2,07,106 ha. Hence, forestry in Nagaland mostly relates to private forests regulated by customary right of the people. The forests, are generally of wet evergreen type with high density and rich in a number of species.

The Nagaland Forest Department have taken up various forestry research works such as (a) setting up of research gardens at different places under different climatic and soil conditions for extensive trial of fast growing tree species to assess their performance in Nagaland (b) laying out increment plot in younger plantation to find out their rate of growth and other relative information. As a result the Department has found three species suitable for Nagaland which while preserving the soil would be of economic value to the people.

The successful breeding of Tragopan Blythe at the Zoological Park in Kohima has drawn world wide reclaim and the London based World Peasant Association has offered to give training to one officer from Nagaland free of cost.

The State has at present two Wild Life Sanctuaries namely Intasgki Wild Life Sanctuary and Public Badze Wild Life Sanctuary.

According to the second All India Census on Tiger held in April 1979 the State has 102 tigers. According to the first such census in 1972 their number was only 80.

Hunting in Govenment reserved forests and shooting of animals like deer, sambhar, elephants, tigers and killing or trapping of tragopan is strictly prohibited throughout the State.

INDUSTRY

In order to industrialise the State the Government opened District Industries Centres in all the seven districts.

The Nagaland Handloom and Handicraft Corporation and Nagaland Khadi and Village Industries Board were also started.

The sericulture farms at Chuchuyimlang and Semaguri have already gone into production. About 1,50,000 Tasar Cocoon have been produced and 10,000 DFLs have been prepared and supplied to the farms as well as to private rearers. About 500 families have been benefitted from this scheme. An amount of Rs. 3 lakhs was spent last year for maintenance of existing farms and new farms are being opened at Akheguo and Kubolong in Phek and Mokokchung Districts respectively.

About 1,200 provisional industrial licences have been issued to small scale industrial units upto last year out of which 100 units have been registered and have gone into production.

Distillery project with daily capacity of 1000 gallons of alcohol was established during 1976-77. The distillery already produced 6 lakh litres of spirit and have already started producing liquor.

The Plywood Factory at Tijut was taken over by the Government from the Saharias for better management last year. The factory has since been revitalised and production is in full swing.

The Rs. 63.13 crore Tuli Pulp & Paper Mill, a joint venture of State Government and H.P.C. is ready for commisoisning. It will provide employment to about 7500 persons when in full operation.

NAGALAND SUGAR MILL

Based on a techno-economic survey conducted by the National Council of Applied Economic Research in 1964-65 and on the advice of the National Sugar Institute, the Nagaland Sugar Mill Co. Ltd. was set up in 1965-66 at Dimapur with a capital outlay of Rs. 237 lakhs and a crushing capacity of 1000 tonnes per day. It was commissioned on 10th March, 1973 and production started on 10th Jan. 1974. It is the second sugar mill in the whole of North Eastern Region of India and the first ever medium size industrial venture set up in Nagaland as public undertaking.

The Mill provides regular employment to 440 persons, seasonal employment to 650 persons and the number of farmers and labourers engaged in sugarcane cultivation is over 6000.

The Mill has paid during 1979-80 over Rs. 103.25 lakh to growers as sugarcane prices. Over the past seven years the Mill had paid about Rs. 175.50 lakh as Central Excise Duty and Sales Tax. There is a growing awareness among farmers of the various facilities offered by banks not only in sugarcane cultivation but in all branches of farming.

NAGALAND STATE TRANSPORT

Nagaland State Transport now covers 30 different routes with passenger bus services with a fleet strength of 205 buses. The longest direct service covering 290 kms. between Mon and Dimapur has been recently opened. Other long distance direct bus services ranging from 145 kms. to 216 kms. are already in operation. Up-to-date facilities and amenities for comfort of passengers are provided at all the bus stations. The department has an allocation of Rs. 1100 lakh including Rs. 245 lakh provided by N.E.C.

POLICE

There are 17 police stations, 15 police out-posts in D.E.F. and under Nagaland Armed Police, there are 69 out posts branching out from the six armed battalions. Under ANP there are 8 check posts.

There is one Police Training Centre for armed police, one signal Training School, and one Police Training School at Chumukedima.

The entire State is covered by four fire service stations.

PHYSICAL EDUCATION

Under physical education there are 21 Rural Sports Centres, two Nehru Yuvak Kendras under Central Government sponsorship and two Youth Centres under State Government.

There are three N.C.C. Companies, 40 Scout troupes, 12 girl guides companies. Financial assistance has been given so far to 45 youth clubs and voluntary sports associations besides giving assistance for construction of 128 play grounds. Over and above this, army has constructed over 60 play-grounds.

So far 1299 kms of surfaced routes, 3,827 kms. unsurfaced routes and 75 buildings, residential and non residential, were constructed last year. After a lapse of three years, the house building loan to government servants has been renewed during 1970-80 and a sum of Rs.12 lakh has been spent benefiting 112 officials while Rs. 5 lakh have been sanctioned under low income scheme benefiting 62 persons last year.

The Centre has sanctioned Rs. 15 lakh under middle income housing scheme for Nagaland this year which will be implemented under 20 point programme for rural areas.

SUPPLY

The working procedure has been streamlined to ensure proper procurement of CPO items, actual delivery of stores at the destination through the introduction of Despatch Signals/ Telegrams and Obtaining confirmation of receipt within 48 hours and proper assessment of the requirement of CPO items by the field officers.

During the year, pattern of supply of CPO items to out post CPO has been changed. In the new system, CPO centres on NST routes are first fed directly by the Central Godown at Dimapur. The interior outpost CPO on Non/NST routes are then fed by employing private contractors who are given indents for lifting of CPO centre on NST routes. This arrangement is effectively followed to ensure that CPO items reach the interior outposts with less changes of malpractices enroute from lifting point to the delivery point. This arrangement has made to prevent all sorts or possible malpractices.

Consequent on entrusting of resonsibility on the Director of Supply for distribution of I/salt in the State, a detailed distribution system has been worked out and all efforts have been made to eliminate possibility of artificial scarcity of I/Salt.

Under the "Food for Work" programme, the Directorate has engaged a large number of unemployed and under employed persons in the rural areas to work on roads, construction of intermediate and main drains etc.

RURAL DEVELOPMENT

It was in 1971, that the rural development programmes were introduced in Nagaland with the establishment of its own unit of EMFDA, when peace prevailed in the State after two decades of sack and slaughter. The villagers still remain underdeveloped, because of lack of communications. Secondly, the activities of the underground elements posed law and order situation. So a large chunk of allotment went to meet the requirement of security. Added to these are the general apathy of the people towards various rural development programmes.

With this background the present Government has formulated and launched a unique, rather a realistic programme for rural development in which the Village Development Board (VDB) would play a major role. The VDB in each village will be exclusively engaged in the development works of the Village Council (VC). The VDBs could be constituted by persons from the Village Council or from the Government service or persons considered eligible, by virtue of their age or tradition or custom, including women as members of the Boards for a period of three years.

The idea of setting up VDB is not new in Nagaland. This practice was followed as a part and parcel of the Naga culture and social polity from time immemorial. In Nagaland, village has got its unique position and today, the Naga population in the State is identified through 1,000 villages.

Under the new scheme the State Government has to give grant-in-aid to every village at the rate of Rs. 200 per household. The total amount of such grant will be deposited with a bank nearest to the respective villages. By the end of Sixth Five

Year Plan at least 50 villages may have sufficient deposit in the bank to undertake their own credit management.

The Government will also apportion a fund to rural development schemes from every department and a certain percentage of the fund so earmarked for rural development will be deposited with the bank for VDSs. To start with, at least 15 per cent of the allocation for rural development will be set aside exclusively for the purpose of grant-in-aid and matching grants.

The State Government has now three-tier Planning Machinery in terms of State Planning Board. District Planning Board and Village Development Board to execute the Scheme at the grass root level.

The two-day Seminar of all the VDB Secretaries and the Chairman of Village Council and Area Council of Nagaland concluded on 22nd May this year at Kohima, which was attended by 2,000 delegates from 900 village ranging from common villagers to ex-underground leaders and ex-Ministers has evoked a spontaneous response of the people to the new time such a massive Seminar of such nature on development programme in the State was called which largely accounts for success.

COOPERATION

Cooperation Department has launched a reorganisation scheme which lay stress on consolidating the existing structure rather then allowing mushroom growth of weak, non-viable co-operative societies. The department also proposes to pay greater attention to the programme for encouraging, specialised activities like handloom, weaving, poultry, piggery, dairy etc. during 1982-83.

Proposed plan provision for the department during 1982-83 is Rs. 43.25 lakh including Rs. 16.25 lakh on centrally sponsored scheme.

MEDICAL AND PUBLIC HEALTH

Five sub-centres dispensaries have been converted into subsidiary health centres during 1981-82 while seen new subsidary health centres and eight new sub-centres have been established. Construction of Food and Drug Laboratory at Kohima and that of a 12 bedded hospital at Pughoboto have been completed. Further programmes to be taken up are construction of 42 sub-centres, two public health centres, one 112 bedded hospital at Sanis, Central Medical Stores at Dimapur, three district medical stores, one District T.B. Centre at Mon and a 40 seated nurses hospital at Mokokchung. Thus at present there are 30 hospitals, 17 public health centres, 69 sub centres, 69 sub-centres, 81 dispensaries, one T.B. and one mental hospital.

Total plan outlay proposed for the department during 1982-83 is Rs. 251.83 lakh which includes Rs. 75.33 lakh as Central Government's share for the centrally sponsored schemes.

WATER SUPPLY

By the end of the current year the target of providing water supply to 108 villages brings the total coverage to 577 villages with a total population of about 4,00,000.

For 1982-83, a total plan provision of Rs. 470 lakhs including Rs. 156 lakh under centrally sponsored schemes had been proposed. During the year, water supply facilities are proposed to be extended to 46 more villages covering a population of about 33,000.

SOCIAL WELFARE

Social Welfare Department has been implementing various schemes for the welfare of children, destitute women, physically handicapped persons and has continued to provide monetary assistance to voluntary organisations. During the current year the scheme of old age pension has been introduced under which the selected beneficiaries get a monthly pension of Rs. 60 per head. This scheme covers all persons from 80 years old and above. The department has also a scheme of granting finanacial assistance to the blind on the line of the Old Age Pension Scheme and special stipends for physically handicapped students.

ART AND CULTURE

With the opening of the Kohima District Library during the proceeding year, the Library services in the State have marked a significant progress. The Library has further been enriched during the year 1981-82. Side by side Research Library and other district libraries are also enriched with considerable number of books.

Three new cultural centres at Phek, Wokha and Zunheboto have just been opened to intensify promotion and preservation of culture like other districts where such organisations were established earlier.

Five more rural libraries are in the process of registrations. This would raise the total number of such libraries under the Directorate of Art and Culture to 40. Assistance in the form of books as before, is being provided to all libraries.

The State Museum is being enriched by adding a variety of specimens. New Diromas, show cases and display cabins have been added. The three cultural centres at Mokokchung, Tuensang and Mon are also continuing to procure specimens of local value for display in portable cabins in the respective centres.

Under Research and Studies, preparations of preliminary reports on the materials and customary laws of two tribes have been completed and circulated during the year under review. The reprinting of the monograph on the Rengma Nagas taken up during the last year is nearing completion.

ARUNACHAL

Arunachal Pradesh had to start from the scratch when the country attained independence. Development of this area is a task requiring huge capital outlay. During the period of Five-Year Plans the Central Government put in all efforts to develop the area in all spheres of economy. The development strategy has been that of rural development with emphasis on agriculture and village industries, provision of water supply, village roads and power generation, education and health services, transport and communication.

MEANS OF COMMUNICATION

Compared to about 1176 kms. of road in 1972, when Arunachal became Union Territory todayth ere are 6,000 kms. of road interlinking various district and sub-divisional headquarters. State Transport buses are new plying on various routes. There are about 194 Post Offices including 28 with telegraph facilities. The Government of India have sanctioned a 12 km. railway line from Balipara to Bhalukpong and two more railway projects, viz., Tipling-Itanagar and Nurkongselek-Pasighat are likely to be sanctioned soon.

BANKS

While there was not a single bank or radio station in the territory in 1947, today there are three radio stations and 18 banks.

ELECTRIFICATION

Arunachal Pradesh is capable of producing half of the hydel potential of the entire country if its innumerable streams are tapped properly. The total installed capacity is now 10,770 Kilowatts. So far 265 villages have been electrified and over a hundred more villages will similarly be benefited soon.

AGRICULTURE

The Administration has been trying to develop the area specially in the field of agriculture by gradual switching over to scientific method of cultivation from the conventional shifting cultivation. The result is very encouraging indeed and the territory is destined to become self-sufficient in food production very soon.

Large chunks of land are being reclaimed and developed for permanent cultivation. The area under high-yielding varieties of cereals are being increased in collaboration with the ICAR Complex. Activities of double-multiple cropping in the usually non-cropped area have been expanded to increase production and horti-cultural activities have becn intensified.

Dirang apples from Arunachal were adjudged the best in the national apple show held last year.

A total number of 25,341 holdings in Arunachal require irrigation and under these holdings, 23,802,077 hectares are irrigated. In Arunachal today there are seven Agricultural farms, two Horticultural People's Nurseries and 744 People's Horticultural gardens. A Regional Apple Nursery has been set up at Dirang with NEC's assistance. Tea, Coffee and cardamom plantations have also sprung up in the territory in recent years.

FOREST WEALTH

In Arunachal Pradesh, the Forest Department realise a revenue of about Rs. 4 crore per annum from the forest products. For the first time, the Forest Department has taken up the Food for Work programme and expect to consume about 200 tonnes of rice and get an additional investment of Rs. 3 lakh worth works. This has proved to be a successful scheme. The Arunachal Pradesh Forest Corporation has been contributing towards development of forest activities. While timber extraction and other operations are being taken up departmenally, it has organised industrial activities by running plywood and saw mills. More than 60 per cent of the area is under forest and development of forestry and forest-based industries has been found feasible, having growth potential. Today, there are 33 forest-based industries in the territory, viz. 18 saw mills, seven veneer mills and seven ply wood factories.

COOPERATIVE MOVEMENT

Co-operative movement in Arunachal Pradesh is a living force and there are at present 114 Co-operative Societies in the territory with about 17,000 members and a working capital of over Rs. 2 crore.

EDUCATION

The pace of enlightenment in Arunachal Pradesh is indeed spectacular. There were only three schools with 50 students on the roll in 1947. And today there are 875 primary schools, 117 middle schools, 26 secondary schools, 10 higher secondary schools, two central schools and two colleges, with nearly 65,001 students on the rolls. At present about six thousand boarders are getting hostel facilities and they are awarded stipends and other amenities. There are about 200 adult education centres in the Territory.

It has been proposed to set up a Regional Institute of Science and Technology in Arunachal Pradesh under the aegis of the North Eastern Council.

DEVELOPMENT OF INDUSTRIES

In the absence of infrastructural factilities industrialisation has been hampered in the Territory despite her abundant natural resources.

The Arunachal Government had meanwhile undertaken survey and preparation of feasibility study project report and consultancy services regarding large and medium scale industries in the territory. The most notable feature of planned programme in the sphere of industrial development is the Government's concerted efforts towards the setting up of Industrial and Financial Corporation with a view to encouraing proper industrial growth in the territory. As indicated in various survey reports, this corporation will evidently remove certain constraints growth.

SMALL SCALE INDUSTRIES

A humble beginning has already been made towards the development of medium and small scale industries. Three medium and 380 village small scale units have been established. So far 25 craft training and 26 production units have been established through which local youths are imparted training in crafts like carpentry weaving, carpet making wood carving, painting, silversmithy tailoring, knitting, sewing, blacksmithy, cane and bamboo works, etc. Moreover, training in motor repair, carpentry, plumbing, wiremanship etc. is imparted to local youths through the existing Industrial Training Institute in the Territory. Utility articles are being produced in local units. The Government is sanctioning 400 stipends every year for local youths who undergo training in various trades they like.

A number of measures have been taken by the Arunachal Pradesh Government to promote growth of industries, for which the Territory has abundant natural resources. The Science and Technology Council was constituted to formulate appropriate plan for growth of industries based on local natural resources and also to suggest suitable technology for harnessing such resources. The Council is expected to help Government in preparing a resource profile based on which specific industrial projects can be taken up. In its first meeting the Council made a number of suggestions relating to survey and assessment of natural resources and their commercial-exploitation. Among important suggestions made by the Council are : (a) quick survey of forest resources to provide industrial data base; (b) preparing plan of action for commercial utilisation of mineral resources and (c) promotion of small-scale industries based on local resources. The Government has initiated action on recommendations of the Council.

Meanwhile feasibility study to set up a fruit canning industries at Basar in Siang District has been completed by the Central Fruit Technological Research Centre. The project is expected to be taken up early.

MINI CEMENT PLANT

The North Eastern Council has sanctioned a thirty-tonne per day capacity mini cement plan at Tezu in Lohit District which will utilise huge deposits of lime stone at Tiding. Preliminary works in this regard have been started. On 26th July, 1980 foundation stone of an industrial unit for manufacturing cheap roofing material utilising wastes, has been laid at Pasight where an Industrial Estate has come up.

The first Industrial Estate of the territory has been started at the capital at Itanagar where about half a dozen local entrepreneurs have successfully started ample scale industrial units.

The Government has been pursuing a plan of raising a 400-hectare tea garden in the joint sector at Basar in East Siang District. Arunachal will soon find a place in the tea map of the country. Efforts are afoot to have yet another cement plant for Arunachal.

Open cast mining and underground mining of coal in Namchik and Nempui area of Tirap District have been undertaken recently and the Mineral Exploration of India have been asked by the North-Eastern Council to mine the same.

One Research and Design Centre has since been established in the territory for revival and revitalisation of local arts and crafts and to conduct research on scientific line with the aim to preserve the local arts and crafts without losing their originality. Meanwhile oil has been struck in the territory and it is proposed to set up a mini refinery at Kharsang in Tirap district soon.

ASSAM

Although agriculture constitutes the major source of Assam's economy with over 80% of her people depending on agriculture directly or otherwise, yet not even 20% of the farmers can manage to have a square meal. Over 87% of the people of this State live in the villages and more then 40% of them are over head and ears in debt. Although Assam's soil is well known for its fertility, the agricultural output had remained at a very low level. One of the reasons being heavy pressure of population on land and lack of enployment opportunity outside agriculture. The size of holdings has become vary small. The average size of operational holding in Assam compares unfavourably with those of the other States of the country.

With the increase of population pressure, new areas have been brought uuder cultivation encroaching upon both forest reserves as well as village grazing reserves thus causing disturbances of the ecological balance. Due to addition of marginal lands, without the application of essential inputs and improved practices, productivity of land has become virtually stagnant.

One of the major causes of the agricultural backwardness perhaps could be attributed to the perennial floods. The mighty river Brahmaputra and the turbulent Aarak, and their tributaries are quite unpredictable in their behaviour. They bring down very large volume of water in the rainy season causing widespread inundation throughout the State, thus causing, on an average, loss of Rs. 10 to 12 crores every year besides taking a huge toll of human lives and cattleheads.

Although Assam has immense natural resources, tea still occupies the dominant position in the industrial era began only with the setting up of the public sector refinery at Gauhati and a fertilizer at Namrup. Her performance in the field of industries is still in its nascent stage with less than 6% of the people depending on industries. Assam has a total tribal population of about 20 lakhs; 4 lakhs in hills and 16 in the plains. Poverty looms large in the hills of Assam with literacy still below 20% and per capita income at the lowest rung of the national ladder. The condition of the hills is causing a major challenge towards the sphere of development of the country.

Although Assam has a vast power potential based on water, natural gas, coal and oil, actual power generation in the State has not even crossed 200 MW mark.

Added to the complexity of Assam's challenge is the growing problem of unemployment. While not many people prefer to go for registration in Employment Exchanges, it is evident that seven lakh persons, both educated and uneducated, are unemployed, while a still larger number of people may be described as underemployed. With the expansion of opportunities for education, a new problem of educated unemployment is visible in Assam giving rise to a variety of socio-economic and political tensions.

With all these problems and complexities, Assam presents a pleasant challenge to the planners for economic development. The North Eastern Council which was set up in 1972, is engaged in the task of helping the constituent units of this region including Assam in coming to grips with their complex problem of backwardness.

Assam is now passing through one of the crucial periods of her history, the people of Assam have before them new challenges and opportunities. Assam's biggest resource lies indeed in her people and her strength stems from human resources and more particularly from younger generation. The Government of India is fully determined to assist Assam and for that matter other units of this region in solving their problems of backwardness. The N.E.C. is also pledged to work for bringing about coordinated and integrated development of this region, of which Assam is a major partner. It is true that Assam would continue to hold the key for prosperity of the whole of north eastern region would never prosper. The challenges are vital, but Assam has the technical back up of the rest of the country available to her through the N.E.C. and a major breakthrough is already in sight. A concerted efforts by various development departments with total support of the people's will and strength will place Assam at per with the most advanced States of the country and make every Assamese a proud partner of the glory that is India.

MANIPUR

Inspite of the continued disturbance from insurgency for the last two decades, Manipur has continued to push on with the efforts of further developmeut and bring about a speedy improvement in the socio-economic life of the people.

One of the important projects already taken up is the centrally sponsored Loktak Multi Purpose Project which is expected to be commissioned in 1982. In addition to this, site for another multipurpose dam at Tipaimukh is being investigated into. These, when commissioned, are expected to become the backbone of agriculture and industrial development of the State. In the industrial field a Khadasari sugar factory with an installed capacity of 60 tons a day and a 25,520 spindled Cotton Spinning Mill have been commissioned. The working group of the Planning Commission has recently approved the proposal for establishment of Starch and Gulcose factory, Sugar factory, Mini-Cement factory and a Mechanised Dye House in Manipur, and action for implementation is already in progress.

Agriculture receives the highest priority. The Loktak Lift Irrigation will irrigate 40,00 acres and the project will enable reclaiming of another 60000 acres of virgin land. Out of the three major irrigation projects, the Khowpum dam has been completed. The Singda dam and the Imphal barrage at the advanced stage of construction.

In addition to these the construction works for the Khuga Irrigation Project and the Theubal Multipurpose project are being taken up.

All the district head quarters and sub-divisional headquadter have been electrified under the Rural Electrification scheme and more villages are being covered every year. Hydro-electric projects at Nungshangkhong in East and Sanahal Lokchao in North District are also at the advanced stage of construction.

With the enforcement of the Official Acts passed, Manipuri Language has become the official language of this state, the Manipur University has come into being, the "Kangla Sha" has been declared as the State Emblem of Manipur and the Meitei script has been recognised.

It is expected that the development works will be accelerated to the maximum once the extremist problem is solved and normal law and order restored.

MEGHALAYA

The urgent task before the Nation today is the progressive reduction in the incidence of poverty and unemplyment. The immediate desire, therefore, is to promote rapid economic development in the country. In Meghalya, conscientious efforts are being made to achieve better development in the rural areas where about 85% of the population live.

Judged from most of the accepted indicators of economic development, Meghalaya lags behind when compared with the other North Eastern States. In comparison with the other States in the country, Meghalaya lags even more behind.

Meghalaya is a state with a predominantly tribal population underlines the special need for adequate and effective measures for the welfare and development of the State. The rural population live in 4583 villages. The villages are small and widely dispersed which makes the provision of infrastructure and social services very expensive. By far, the largest number of poor people live in the rural areas. The people who constitute the unemployed in the State belong mostly to the category of the rural underemployed. Most of the people in the rural areas and a substantial portion of the population in the urban areas subsist below the poverty line. Agriculture and allied activities remain the most dominant sector of the State economy. The wasteful method of shifting cultivation or jhumming acts as a limiting factor against growth of the economy in the rural areas. The economic development of the people living in the border areas is yet to reach the take-off stage. Having a long border with Bangladesh, discontiuance of the traditional channels of trade after partition had badly disrupted the economy of the area. The road communication facilities in the State are extremely underdeveloped which pushes up the costs of execution of development schemes.

These are some of the factors which act as constraints in the development of the State and in particular, the rural areas.

Meghalaya became a full-fledged state only in the year 1972 and, therefore, the fourth Five Year Plan was the first plan for the State. Development of this area in the earlier plans formed part of the composite Assam State Plan. In spite of the development programme taken up in the past, much remains to be done, particularly in the lessdeveloped rural areas of the State. The concentration of development in Meghalaya as elsewhere in the country, has been seen mostly in the urban areas. Inspite of the best intentions, the benefits of development had percolated only slowly to the rural areas. The impact of investment in the rural areas was not retained in the rural areas to the extent in the manner desired. This led to the continuous migration to the towns from the villages.

Rural poverty is reflected in poor nutrition, inadequate shelter and low health standards. These, in turn, affect the productivity of the rural poor and their quality of life. Economic development is not equitably reaching the poor in this State and the poor are not significantly contributing to the growth. Development strategies, therefore, need to be redesigned so as to help the poor to become more productive. In this context the Government of Meghalaya is emphasising the programme of approach of growth with social justice.

Realising the fact that development of rural activities is dependent upon a well-planned road net work, the State Government is giving maximum importance on construction of roads to connect the rural areas with consumption centres. The rural road system will connect villages with central places, market centres and other centres providing a wide range of functions needed for development of agriculture, horticulture, forestry, animal husbandry and sericulture.

Along with developing resource potential, infrastructure and economic activities, the state's development programme emphasises development of local human capital in rural areas and changing the socio-economic framework in which this resource functions. For this, an integrated strategy of development of rural areas during the Sixth Plan period has been drawn up. This strategy consists of the following main thrusts—(1) development programme aimed at agricultural production and productivity including development of irrigation facilities, soil conservation with emphasis on control of jhumming, provision of modern agriculture inputs at reasonable prices, improving agricultural marketing facilities as also educating the farmers in new agricultural techniques; (2) Since authentic land records are not available in most areas of the State, steps are also being taken to cadastrally survey the State; (3) development of activities allied to agriculture like dairying, poultry keeping, animal husbandry, forestry, fishery development of a public distribution system to supply essential consumer goods to people at reasonable rates; (5) setting up of cottage and small scale and village industries including sericulture and handloom weaving with a view to providing employment all round the year.

Since the local people have strong community feeling and long traditions of democratic institutions, the cooperative movement and the village level institutions have a tremendous scope of success. The development strategy for the future years takes this important factor into account. With a view to sustaining the programmes of economic development in the State, local people are being encouraged to take up trades and business through the Trade Centre Scheme. Side by side, special programme for rejuvenating the economy of border areas and to wean away jhummias to settled type of cultivation have been launched.

A new strategy of integrated rural development through micro—level planning has been evolved by the Government of India. This is intended to bring about an overall economic development of the block area encompassing all aspects of the economy, namely, primary, secondary and teritiary. This beneficiary oriented scheme is also being implemented in Meghalaya along with the other ongoing rural programmes.

Besides development efforts, training of local personnel is of crucial importance. The State Government is keen to train the local boys and girls in various technical and skilled trades and steps are being taken in this regard.

Development and availability of social facilities are closely related. The need for providing social facilities in rural areas has been recognised and operational guidelines for providing these facilities have been laid down in the form of Minimum Needs Programmes which are being implemented and will be continued with vigour.

To get the Meghalayan economy out of the present state of stagnation it would require continuous and concerted efforts over the years to come. In order to match the physical resources and its command on the one hand, the aim of development for the State is to catch up with the rest of the country in per capita income by the shortest possible period. The task is no doubt stupendous and the time is short but it is by no means insurmountable. Owing to the late start, the level of investment, hence plan outlay, in Meghalaya for the next plan period will have to be such as would help the realisation of this objective of bringing the Meghalayan economy closer to that of the rest of India. Since the State's own financial resources are negligible compared to its needs, funds for increased outlays will have to come from the Government of India and financial institutions.

MIZORAM

The Union Territory of Mizoram was inaugurated by the Prime Minister Shrimati Indira Gandhi at Aizawl on the 21st January, 1972. The event marked the birth of Mizoram as a distinct entity in the large family of the Indian nation and it was celebrated with great enthusiasm all over Mizoram.

The picturesque Mizoram, formerly known as the Lushai Hills District was attached to Assam while the South Lushai Hills District formed part of Bengal. In 1818, the two districts were amalgamated and brought under Assam as one district. Again with the implementation of the North Eastern reorganisation Act (1971), Mizo District ceased to be part of Assam and became a Union Territory under a new name MIZORAM. Mizoram now has a popular government with a Legislature of its own, with a Cabinet and the Lieutenant Governor is the Administrator. The word "Mizo" refers to the people and 'ram' to the land. More than 90% of the Mizos are Christians and of Mongoloid stock.

Perched like a lone sentinel on the tip of the North Eastern border of India and lying between 22°19' and 24°19' N and 92°16 and 93°26' E, Mizoram has an area of 21,090 sq. km. with a population of 3,32,390. Mizoram can boast of a very high percentage of literacy of 54% which is surpassed only by Chandigarh, Kerala and Delhi.

Mizoram, bounded on the east and south by Burma and on the west by Bangladesh, now forms one of the imporant strategic states of N.E. India and is determined to forge ahead under the dynamic leadership of the Prime Minister Indira Gandhi.

With the new political dispensation in Mizoram the benefits of the new economic programme resulted in the improvement of law and order situation. The recent peace accord arrived at between the Government of India and the underground hostiles ushers in a new chapter of peace and progress in Mizoram.

TRIPURA

Smallest but one State in size in the country (except Sikkim), Tripura is a land-locked State. The only road connected to the State, and that too not yet fully stabilised, is through North Bengal, Assam and Meghalaya. It has only 17 km of Railway line within the territory. The road connections and communications in the interior are still underdeveloped. Topographically, the State is so placed that natural calamities like flood and drought are regular features. 84% of the total boundary of the State is with Bangladesh.

The population of the State consists mainly of refugees from erstwhile East Pakistan (now Bangladesh) and tribal Jhumias. The former did not have any economic rehabilitation worth its name, the latter still depend on traditional jhum cultivation. As a result, the economic base of the people of the State is too weak. 41.4% of the population of the State belong to scheduled Caste/scheduled Tribe communities. In this State, we find now 81.8% of the population below poverty line. According to the information furnished before the Rajya Sabha on 27.11.80 Tripura is one of the nine states in the country and one of two states in the North Eastern Region, having higher percentage of people below poverty line than the national average.

The State is basically agarian, though 60%of its total area of 10,477 sq. km is hilly and mountaneous. About 77 percent of the working force depend on Agriculture which constitutes 63 per cent of State domestic product, More than 89% of the people live in villages. The operational holding is however too small. Out of total operational holding of 2.5 lakhs, more than 1.14 lakhs holdings are below 0-5 hectares, 0.58 lakhs holdings are below 1.0 hectares. Even though agriculture still dominates the economy yet its contribution to State domestic product has remained almost the same over the years. The jhumia tribals still practice old jhum cultivation. While people mainly follow single crop pattern, areas under high yielding varieties and multiple cash crops is yet to pick up. Assured irrigation is availale only for about 10 per cent of the cultivable land. For sustaining agricultural development 'Land Reforms' is an important aspect, particularly for a State where Barga system covers a large percent of cultivable areas. The revision survey, the registration of Bargadars, and recording of rights of Bargadars have just been taken up.

The growth of the non-agricultural sector has too low. The percentage of workers in non-agriculture sector rose by about 0.8 percent only over about a decade. This is for the reason that no major or medium industry grew in the State. At the same time small and cottage industries/handicrafts etc. of the State, though of exquisite qualifies continued to suffer from various ailments. There has been no Public Sector or Private sector enterprise in the State.

The greatest bottlenecks in the developmental activities of the State is the transport. It is necessary to extend railway line from Dharmanagar to Kumarghat and then to Sabroom via Agartala without further loss of time. At present, the States of Tripura and Mizoram as also Cachar district of Assam are catered by the Lumding-Badarpur section of N.F. Rly with its limited capacity. The present load-bearing capacity of this section is too meagre for the need. It is necessary to make it double line operative section on priority basis.

Substantial investments are necessary to ensure diversification and multiplicity of crops, extensive cultivation of high yielding varietites activisation of the Tea-gardens, starting of more medium irrigration projects, starting raw-materials-based industry like paper imll, as recommended by Dinesh Singh Committee of the Parliament, starting of small local industries which have good local market (bakery, spinning mill, biscuit making factory, etc.)

This State (as also the State of Mizoram and Cachar District of Assam) face difficulties not only in importing essential articles, but also in marketing the products. As suggested by the Dinesh Singh Committee of the Parliament, a common marketing and supply corporation for the region my be started immediately. The said committee also recommended establishment of North Eastern Industrial Development Corporation (for setting up of thermal and chemical complexes, etc. based on local raw materials) and North Eastern-Development Bank (to provide institutional finance). These also need to be expedited. The Dinesh Singh Committee made a number of suggestions for quicker/speedier economic development of the State. It is necessary to take measures for implementation of all these recommendations for ensuring speedier economic development of Tripura. The problems of Tripura arising out of economic backwardness can be tackled by taking on priority basis the following recommendations of the Committee :—

(a) A special cropping programme with sufficient investment should be undertaken to develop and utilise the undulated up-lands·

(b) Larger investments should be made in Tea, Jute and Rubber with special objective to transform unsettled tribals into a society based on plantation;

(c) Greater investments should be made in the sector of sericulture with ideas to resettle landless and homeless agriculturists, particularly tribal jhumias.

Development of subsidiaries and manufacturing centres for silk production could also be considered.

(d) Increased allocation of fund should be made for development of the forestry sector which will result in improving earning capacities of the tribal poor living in and around forests and also ensure settled occupations for them.

(e) A really large road building proagrmme should be undertaken.

(f) Micro-hydel projects should be taken up to assure supply of power needed,

(g) Cargo or passenegr-cargo air service between Calcutta and Aagrtala at concessional rate should be introduced to enable marketing of Tripura products in Calcutta.

(h) More rapid economic development of scheduled tribes, Scheduled castes and other weaker section of the people sould be ensured.

(i) Liberal and sufficient availability of consumption and operational credit to the farmers/weaker section should be ensured.

(j) Extensive and useful implementation of Food for work Programme (since changed as National Rural Employment Programme) to provide employments to rural unemployed.

(k) Schemes should be undertaken to provide sufficiently attactive self-employment schemes to educated unemployed,

(l) Schemes should be undertaken to energies the handloom and handicrafts sectors.

With the State returning fast to normalcy, and with effective and quicker measures on all the items and aspects discussed above, we hope that economic development of Tripura and solution of its problems may not be an impossible task.

9. A typical village setting in Arunachal Pradesh

10A. Assamese women with baskets plucking tea leaves

10B. Harvesting in Meghalaya

11A. Meghalaya cloth

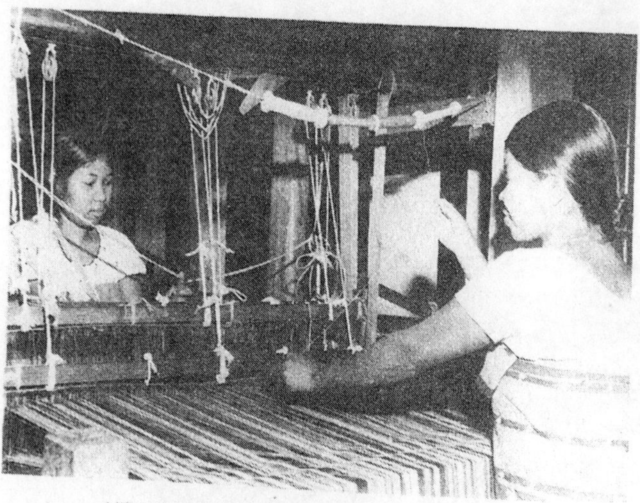

11B. Weavers of Meghalaya busy at work

12. A craftsman at work

13A. An Assamese woman playing a charkha

13B. A Manipuri woman busy at weaving

14. An Assemese weaver at work

15A. A craftsman at work in Assam

16. Typical temple in Assam

17A. A new bridge built in Pashighat

17B. Suspension bridge of Itanagar in Arunachal Pradesh

18A. Tug of war—Manipur style

18B. Polo game being played in Imphal

19A. Singers of Assam

19B. Dancers of Nagaland of Santam tribe

20A. Women of Assam enjoying dancing

20B. Manipuri dancers

21A. Raslila of Manipur

21B. Raslila of Manipur